"With bliss-filled joy, I ai
Dahl's book *Raising Spirit-Led Kids.* Packed with practical
tools, biblical insight and firsthand testimonies from empowered families, *Raising Spirit-Led Kids* offers great wisdom from
Seth's many years of experience as a ministry leader and as a
father."

Georgian Banov, president and co-founder, Global Celebration

"Seth Dahl is among the few who know how to couple the heart
of a child with the realities of heaven. I've loved working along-
side him as he trained children to know a loving Father, hear
His voice and trust Him to lead them in life. He's done such a
beautiful job of translating what many adults stumble on, into
fun, life-giving lessons. *Raising Spirit-Led Kids* is a perfect book
for Seth to introduce to the Body of Christ! He is just the guy
to help us all simplify, as Jesus did, the will of the Father into
ways to love each other better. This book is a gift to any parent who wants to open the eyes of their child to a Kingdom of
power, miracles and wonders. I highly recommend this book to
help guide you in parenting a child in 'the way they should go.'"

Danny Silk, author, *Loving Our Kids On Purpose*, *Keep Your
Love On* and *Unpunishable*

"*Raising Spirit-Led Kids* is such a timely and powerful resource
for parents, grandparents or anyone working with children.
Seth does a phenomenal job of shaping perspective and offering
practical steps on how we can all lead our children into a more
powerful walk with God. Over and over I have found that the
biggest determining factor of kids encountering God is whether
or not they have an adult in their life who nurtures their spirit
in freedom and faith. This book will give you the tools to be
that adult in your child's life."

Jennifer Toledo, senior pastor, Expression 58 Church,
Los Angeles; author, *Children and the Supernatural*

"*Raising Spirit-Led Kids* is such a precious and weighty gift being given to the earth right now through Seth Dahl. It's full of practical tips, biblical wisdom, testimony and experience that will be a powerful tool for parents raising children. This book will assist people in raising world changers in Christ. Thank you, Seth, for penning this incredible treasure chest of heavenly wisdom."

Lana Vawser, author, speaker, prophetic voice,
Lana Vawser Ministries

RAISING
SPIRIT-LED
KIDS

RAISING SPIRIT-LED KIDS

GUIDING KIDS TO WALK
NATURALLY IN THE SUPERNATURAL

SETH DAHL

Chosen

a division of Baker Publishing Group
Minneapolis, Minnesota

Published by Chosen Books
11400 Hampshire Avenue South
Bloomington, Minnesota 55438
www.chosenbooks.com

Chosen Books is a division of
Baker Publishing Group, Grand Rapids, Michigan

Printed in the United States of America

ISBN 978-0-8007-9998-4 (paper)
ISBN 978-0-8007-6219-3 (casebound)

Library of Congress Control Number: 2020943525

In some cases, the identifying details of individuals have been changed to protect privacy.

20 21 22 23 24 25 26   7 6 5 4 3 2 1

CONTENTS

Acknowledgments 9
Foreword by Bill Johnson 11
Introduction 15

PART ONE BUILDING WITH GOD
1. The House That God Builds 23
2. The Way They Should Go 35
3. Stay a Novice 43

PART TWO THE SPIRIT-GUIDED PARENT
4. Raising Sons and Daughters 59
5. Dreaming with God 73
6. Do Not (Always) Tell the Truth 83

PART THREE SPIRIT-FILLED CHILDREN
7. Learning God's Alphabet 99
8. Children Who See 111
9. Exercising Our Senses 121

10. Word Becoming Flesh   137
11. They Have Been with Jesus   145

PART FOUR CONCLUSION

12. Staying Hungry   155
13. Fighting and Building   163

ACKNOWLEDGMENTS

To Lauren, Molly and Abigail for helping edit and fine-tune the content of this book. To the parents who have allowed me to speak into their families and help with their kids. To all my leaders and pastors who have helped make me the Christian that I am, as well as the husband and father that I am. To my children who have taught me so much about being a child of God. Thank you from my whole heart.

FOREWORD

The Israelites were given instructions on how to keep the supernatural interventions of God at the forefront of their minds. To help with this assignment, they were to keep their miracle history as a vibrant part of their conversation. They were to rehearse the stories continuously to their children. By doing so, they would pass down more than a shared bank of memories. These testimonies—repeated again and again—would build an infrastructure in the mindsets and values of their children. This was so that there could be another generation who lived with both an awareness of God's presence and an understanding of His character. Future generations would then inherit the legacy of their parents' relationship with the God of promises, thus establishing an expectation for His goodness upon which they would build their lives. In this way, the Israelites would inhabit their promised land in the way God intended.

The principle that good stewardship invites increase is a Kingdom principle that is applicable in every area of our lives. God chose to give Himself to the Israelites as an inheritance, as He did with us, but it was the job of the parents to train their children into the awareness and stewardship of that gift.

We can and do outsource the task of training our children to trusted teachers, coaches and pastors. But the role of guiding our children in their relationship with God lays first and foremost at our feet. No matter what else I choose to do with my days, my family is the first church that I pastor.

Raising Spirit-Led Kids is built upon this premise. God has gifted uniquely each parent, grandparent and caregiver to stir up the hunger for God in the children under their care. Psalm 78 speaks of an entire generation coming to know their identity "that they should put their confidence in God" (Psalm 78:7 NASB). That is what this book is working toward.

Seth Dahl was an integral part of the Bethel team for over ten wonderful years. His impact is felt to this day. During his time with us, children and families were given the freedom to explore their relationship with the Holy Spirit and with the power of the supernatural. We believe so deeply that there is no junior Holy Spirit that if a difficult cancer case needs healing, we will often send that case to the kids. If a leadership team is hungry to hear from God, it is often the elementary school that gets enlisted. When the glory clouds first manifested during a Bethel service, none of the adults knew what to do. There was not any manual for such an experience! But the kids knew. Without any hesitation, they ran into the manifestation of His presence with outstretched arms, dancing and laughing. When children have been empowered to explore the fullness of their relationship with God, we demonstrate wisdom when we follow their lead.

Raising Spirit-Led Kids is filled with practical tools, biblical insights and firsthand testimonies of families who were empowered to grab ahold of all that the Lord has for their children. Seth offers wisdom gleaned from his many years of experience in ministry working with thousands of families, but also from his experience as a father to his own children. Children were always meant to be an integral part of a family's Kingdom assignment on the earth. They are "arrows in the hands of a warrior" (Psalm 127:4 NIV). As Seth writes, "No warrior can afford to enter a battle with arrows he did not help shape." I would encourage every person involved in raising children to read this book. Let it inspire and challenge you to take the reins of your children's spiritual training, building within them an awareness of God's presence until we can inhabit our promised land—on earth as it is in heaven.

Bill Johnson,
Bethel Church, Redding, California,
author of *Raising Giant-Killers* and *The Way of Life*

INTRODUCTION

My first four years ministering to children were spent in the projects of New York City. On average, we would have 200 children attend our outdoor Sunday School services. We would arrive and set tarps down on the sidewalk for the kids to sit on, and then we would grab a stack of fliers and wait outside their school. The fliers had pictures of our logo and the candy the kids would receive after attending Sunday School.

We did this regardless of what the weather was. Sometimes it was over ninety degrees and humid, and other times it was below freezing. We believed that if the drug dealers showed up no matter the weather to try to corrupt these kids, we would show up and preach the Gospel.

Once the school bell rang, it was mere seconds before the sidewalks were flooded with children. We passed out our fliers excitedly and announced our event loudly to the children who had slipped past us without grabbing one. The entire time someone would stay with the truck, blast music and use the microphone to invite kids to come join us on the sidewalk. As soon as the rush died down, the people passing out fliers would head back to the truck and prepare to start the first service.

When it was hot, we played water games to keep everyone cool. When it was cold and our hands were frozen to the microphones, we served hot chocolate and steaming cups of noodles to kids and parents. Many times, the kids would sit on the tarps and the parents would sit on benches behind them. Drug deals were happening quite consistently around us as we ministered. Sometimes it was even the parents who participated in the drug deals. They took the opportunity of their kids being occupied to make a little money.

We did this five days a week, and most days we had two or three separate services. As soon as we finished one, we would drive to a different housing community and start again. Between the seventeen teams doing this simultaneously and the 3,000 kids we brought to the church on Saturdays, we reached an average of 20,000 children per week. Many days we only stopped when it was too dark to continue.

While this was a satisfying and powerful time of ministry, I felt led to make a change. I left New York and moved to Redding, California. A few years earlier I had been saved radically and delivered from drugs, so I knew that God could do incredible things—I just was not seeing it very often. I felt led to go somewhere I could see God move in power and learn how to experience that for myself.

I spent the following ten years in Redding both learning and ministering. I created a Sidewalk Sunday School program for the children who lived in trailer parks and low-income housing areas. While the services were much smaller than the ones I had facilitated in New York, the goal was the same: reach as many children as possible. I combined what I brought from New York with what I was learning in Redding. Because of that, we saw the children begin to walk with God in ways that most adults only dream of.

We saw children pray for a homeless man who had destroyed one of his knees. Moments later he was sprinting across a baseball field. We saw children pray for one of their friends who had warts all over her hands, and within days they were gone completely. Another girl had torn something in her shoulder and could not lift her arm. During worship, she heard God tell her to lift her arm and follow along with the hand motions of the song. After she argued back and forth with God a few times, telling Him that she could not lift her arm, she finally tried it. Whatever she had torn was healed. Her parents told us that when she got home, she was even able to do pull-ups. A boy who had been suffering from many daily seizures was set free instantly. This happened as the children gathered around him and told the seizures to leave him alone in Jesus' name. During these years, we also saw countless children get filled with the Holy Spirit, oftentimes needing to be carried out of the service because they were overcome by His presence. The stories go on and on.

I began to travel to other cities and nations teaching children's ministers what we had learned about children and God. During a ministry trip to England, I became friends with one of the other speakers. Over a meal she mentioned casually that there were several things that many children's pastors do in church that she never would. One of those things was praying for children to be filled with the Holy Spirit. She had my attention, since the whole reason I was there to speak was because of the things we saw in our church that she was now telling me she would never do. When I asked her why, she told me she could never rob the parents of being part of those beautiful experiences. My mind was blown, and I have pondered that conversation ever since.

A little while later, I was invited to Austria to lead a conference that had both children and parents in attendance. Up until that point, I had focused my time on training other children's workers. I had never done anything that included both parents and children, and I was nervous. I planned the days to be similar to what I would have done if I had been ministering to children's workers, but instead of leading the children's workers in the ministry and activation times, I would lead the parents as if they were the ministry team to their own children.

I will never forget what happened during those four days. In all of my years as a children's pastor, I have never seen anything as powerful. Parents and children experienced God deeply together. During one of the sessions, the children and parents wrote down their sins, the feelings those sins created, and any names they had taken as an identity due to those actions and feelings. They then brought their papers up to the stage where we had placed a cross, and the families left their papers and everything written on them at the cross.

Shortly after, a young boy with his grandmother came to me weeping. Through a translator he told me that he wanted to give his life to Jesus. I explained that by bringing those things to the cross, he had given his life to Jesus already, and now Jesus wanted to give His life to the young boy. We took a couple of minutes and prayed for him as the Lord filled him with the life and love of God.

After another session about engaging our hearts as we read the Bible, a young girl remained on the floor weeping while many of the other children went to get a snack. We asked her what was going on, and she told us that she could not transition to the next thing because she had seen and heard Jesus. The tears, joy and gratitude from these families shook me to my core.

On the flight home, a thought passed through my mind that sounded almost blasphemous for a children's pastor. *I do not know if I believe in children's church anymore.* As I got past the shock of that thought, I began to process how and why I had arrived at this way of thinking. For the first time in years of ministry, I was seeing a few important truths. One was that ministry should first be experienced in the home. This is where children should encounter Jesus on a regular basis. Another truth was that parents are the first pastors. In all the years of equipping leaders, I had not been utilizing or training the most important leaders of all.

I had spent years working to change the church's mindset regarding children's ministry by communicating with passion that the purpose of children's church is teaching and training, not simply babysitting. I had spent years traveling, teaching and filming to shift this perception—and now I was the one who needed a change of perspective.

God continued to unpack this revelation to me. One day as I was in a sporting goods store looking at bows and arrows, He brought a Scripture verse to mind. "Like arrows in the hand of a warrior, so are the children of one's youth. How blessed is the man whose quiver is full of them" (Psalm 127:4–5 NASB). He pointed out that if I wanted to, I could pick out a package of arrows and take them to the counter. They were perfectly straight, razor sharp, and for fifty dollars they could be mine.

He helped me realize I had been looking at church like a sporting goods store with the children's church as the archery aisle. I had been working under the paradigm that if parents dropped their kids off and gave their tithes and offerings, then it was the responsibility of the children's ministry team to package their "arrows" (children) for them so that they would fly straight and hit the mark. I believe that many people view children's ministry this way.

There were no sporting goods stores when Psalm 127 was written, of course. Warriors could not run in and buy their arrows in packs. They were, instead, required to shape their own arrows. They had a significant part to play not only in learning their arrows intimately, but also shaping them to be the weapons they were meant to be.

In the same way, parents cannot pick up their children from church and expect them to fly straight and hit the mark. They play a massive role in the spiritual development of their own children. As parents, our role in our children's spiritual lives is more important than anyone else's. We are the ones who aim and release them into their destinies.

I do still believe in children's church and in Christian schools, but I do not believe that parents are meant to delegate the full responsibility of their children's spiritual lives to anyone else. Like ancient warriors would have partnered with other skilled craftsmen to create the best arrowhead possible, parents should work with the church and the school to craft their arrows. The church can give parents a sharp tip, the school can attach the fletching that they need, but the overall shaping of the arrow is the role of the warrior.

In ancient times, this was a matter of life and death. It is the same today. We cannot afford to pick our kids up from school or church and believe that from those institutions alone they will be ready to stop the enemy. No warrior can afford to enter a battle with arrows he did not help shape.

From these three experiences, my entire focus in ministry changed. It was from these experiences that the ideas communicated in this book were born. As parents, we have long-range weapons of the spirit realm in our own homes. As we discover how to first minister *to* our children and then *with* our children, we are both shaping them to be who God designed them to be and doing damage to the kingdom of darkness. Good archers have always been able to change the course of a battle. The goal of this book is the same: to help you learn how to alter the spiritual battle of our world once and for all.

One book could not contain all of the lessons that I have learned during sixteen years of full-time children's ministry. What is written in this book, however, is enough to function as a springboard to propel you and your children deeper into the things of God.

PART 1

BUILDING WITH GOD

1

THE HOUSE THAT GOD BUILDS

TRUE CULTURE

Working in the church, I spent a lot of time discovering, discussing, and creating culture. Danny Silk, who serves on the leadership teams of both Bethel Church in Redding, California, and Jesus Culture in Sacramento, California, teaches that in order to truly have a church culture, you must be able to see similarities in every area of the church. If you go into the main adult service, for example, and you observe that people are being ministered to and receiving healing, you should look at all of the facets of the church before you decide if this is a church with a culture of healing. You should observe the various ministries, such as the nursery, the youth department, the senior citizen gatherings and the outreach ministries to see if healings are taking place in all areas. If they are, the church has a culture of healing. If they are not, they do not have a culture of healing; instead, they have a main service in which people may receive healing.

The culture inside the church is important, because this is how the saints are equipped for the work of ministry. The congregation learns what is available, and if they are paying attention, they can learn much about walking and working with God. But if what happens inside the church does not have an impact on the everyday lives of the congregation, then the culture modeled on Sunday morning remains merely a church culture. This is not what God intended for us as believers.

Jesus did not teach us to pray, "In church as it is in heaven," but rather, "On earth as it is in heaven" (Matthew 6:10). What we learn and witness in church that looks and feels like heaven should go with us everywhere.

Jonathan Welton, who directed the Welton Academy and has written several books, including *Understanding the Whole Bible*, teaches that the word *culture* can best be defined as "a lifestyle." This means that we only know what our culture is by the way we live our lives, not by the notes we take during a sermon or how we behave when we get out of our car to walk into church.[1] I would even go as far as to say that if I walk with my family from the car into church in a different manner than how I get them from the house to the car, I do not have a consistent family culture—I have performance. I am acting a certain way in front of the people at my church so that they will think I have incorporated the church's culture. In reality, though, I have not.

When our children see this, we are modeling for them a false Christianity. Instead of imparting the Kingdom of God, we could end up teaching them event-based religiosity. They might grow up believing that being a Christian is something that they do only on Sunday mornings and during the mid-week services. They could understand our faith as being something that they are to turn on and off—depending upon who they are with or

1. Jonathan Welton, "Supernatural Bible School," *Welton Academy*, 2 June, 2017, https://weltonacademy.com/.

what building they are in—rather than having it define who they are. If this happens, we will have turned our efforts to disciple our children into vain labor.

In order to nurture the authentic culture of the Kingdom of God in our children, our Christianity must leave the building. We are doing our part to shape our arrows if our children witness our lives outside of church lining up with what they have heard and sung about in church. They will see how the verses they learned in Sunday School fit into their everyday lives just as the arrowhead fits the spine of the arrow. In other words, when our beliefs leave the church building, we begin building with God.

BUILDING WITH GOD

The good news is that we do not have to adapt a false Christianity, no matter how many generations before us did. We are given the incredible promise that it is possible to build our homes with God in a way where nothing we do is in vain. "Unless the LORD builds the house, they labor in vain who build it" (Psalm 127:1 NASB).

The phrase *in vain* is such an interesting use of words. The English definition of the phrase means to be "ineffectual or unsuccessful; without real significance, value, or importance." When the Lord builds our house, it is not built with concern for the external appearance. We do not put on a show.

The Hebrew word used is even stronger than in English. It carries the sense that what we are doing is empty, worthless and false. None of us wants to build our homes in a manner that would utilize either of these definitions. We do not want to build in vain; we want to build with God.

Building our family life in partnership with God is similar to the relationship that exists between architects and contractors. Contractors need their blueprints from an architect. With blueprints, the contractor can build what the architect designed. We are God's contractors for our homes, building together with Him to create what He intended. Here are three things that we need to know as contractors who are working with the Architect of our homes.

1) "Newer does not necessarily mean better."[2] At the end of the 19th century, asbestos became the new thing to include in the construction of buildings. It had such desirable physical properties that many contractors wanted to include it. Asbestos absorbs sound, is resistant to fire, heat, electricity and is very affordable. Fortunately, we discovered that asbestos can also cause serious and fatal illnesses. Unfortunately, however, we found this out long after we had included it in the construction of many buildings. Currently, asbestos is estimated to cause 255,000 deaths per year.[3] Even now, we are still trying to remove asbestos from buildings built over 100 years ago. In construction, just because something is new, affordable or convenient does not mean we should use it. It has not stood the test of time. It is the same in our families. Just because something is new and convenient does not mean it is God's plan for us, and convenience should not always be a deciding factor in how we build our families. Similarly, just because authorities are doing something new as they build their families does not mean we need to adopt those methods as we build ours.

2) "Focus on the details. Architects spend long hours measuring, drawing, and re-measuring to produce precise

2. South Bay Construction, "Building Better Relationships: What Contractors Wish Architects Knew About Construction," accessed 13 October, 2016, https://www.sbci.com/architect-contractor-relationship/.

3. *Wikipedia*, s.v. "Asbestos," last modified 13 March, 2020, https://en.wikipedia.org/wiki/Asbestos.

angles and other specifications. Though this work may be laborious, the precision is vital to the success of every project, no matter how big or small. Contractors have to execute the architects' specifications as precisely as they can."[4] The more details contractors receive from the architect, the better they can do. Similarly, the more we look into God's Word and bring our challenges to Him in prayer, the more we see His blueprint for our family. We see this with Moses. God laid out for him the exact details of how he was to build the tabernacle, which was the dwelling place for God among His people (see Exodus 25:9).

3) The relationship between architect and contractor is of absolute importance. God entrusts us to bring to life the vision He has for our homes. "A poor architect-contractor relationship may result in . . . delayed construction, exceeded budgets, or even an unfinished building."[5] Our communication with God is essential in building our homes. Like Jesus, we want to only do what we see the Father doing, and He loves us so much He is willing to show us His entire plan (see John 5:19–20; 1 Corinthians 2:9–10). He is more than happy to help us, to speak to us and to remind us of verses or stories that He has shown us so that we execute on earth what He designed in heaven.

CREATING CULTURE

How do we create true culture in our homes? I once heard someone say that children are really bad at doing what they are told

4. South Bay Construction, "Building Better Relationships: What Contractors Wish Architects Knew About Construction," accessed 13 October, 2016, https://www.sbci.com/architect-contractor-relationship/.
    5. Ibid.

but really good at doing what they are shown. Another way to say that is that the Christian life is better caught than taught. If we want our children to grow up with a thriving relationship with God, the best thing we can do is to demonstrate our relationship with God to them. We must keep in mind that we are always teaching, and we often teach more to our children in those times we do not realize that we are teaching.

One night I went into our daughter's room while she was sleeping and prayed for her future husband. I prayed that God would protect this young man's purity as he moved into adolescence. I prayed that he would love her deeply and watch over her for her entire life.

As I prayed this, I felt Him say to me that I needed to be that same type of husband to her mother. I needed to demonstrate to my daughter the character of the husband I was praying that she would look for. I also needed to be the type of husband I wanted my sons to grow up and become.

In the same way, I want to show my children what it looks like to be a believer so that as they make their own decisions in life they will have something accurate from which to decide. There are too many children who walk away from their definition of Christianity as they grow up. It is more difficult to walk away from a life of intimacy and power than it is to walk away from a life warming a pew.

EDUCATION THROUGH DEMONSTRATION

As a children's pastor, I would ask different children each week to pray. The leaders and I began to notice that when children prayed, it was as if we were seeing into their homes and watching how their parents prayed. One week a child would come to the microphone to pray for the lesson, but they would pray almost as if they were praying for dinner. Another week, a child would start binding all of the demons in the room. The next week a child would pray quietly in simple trust talking to his good, caring Father. Some would pray as if they were reading a checklist of things they needed to cover in every prayer, even if we were not praying for anything remotely related to their list. Oftentimes, we would teach something simple and clear about prayer. We would say, for example, "We don't need to beg God for healing as if we need to convince Him. He is listening. We have His attention. Healing is His will and His idea, so we don't beg, we declare." We would bring some kids up to pray using the directive we had taught, and sure enough, some would pray in ways that were drastically different from what we had just taught. We were simply hearing their parents' nightly prayers come out.

We witnessed the power of culture right before our eyes. We watched as the culture of their homes overwrote the teaching that the children had received. Time and time again we would remind kids of what we had just taught, and then help guide them a little by giving them words to repeat. Our goal was to show the children a different way of praying so that they could introduce it into their homes. We knew that if this important aspect of children's ministry was successful, then we would have a chance of creating a new normal within each child's home.

We gave children room to practice the things they were taught. We believed that they would have the ability to shape the culture of their homes if the principles that we taught made their way into the kids' hearts. This happened with a family whose dog became seriously ill. They took him to the vet for X-rays where they found out that he had eaten the plastic handles off of a pair of scissors. His entire digestive system was blocked. Over the next few days, the dog got worse. He was not eating or drinking and was deteriorating rapidly. As the time approached when it looked like the dog was on the verge of death, the family gathered around him crying.

All of a sudden, their four-year-old son asked the family why they were crying instead of praying. He reminded them that they had been taught what to do, but they were not doing it. The family adjusted instantly. The mom and one of the daughters started drawing prophetic pictures of the dog, the dad and another daughter started to worship, the third daughter started dancing and the young boy started to declare life over his dog. Within minutes, the dog jumped up, ran outside, passed the plastic, drank some water and ate a meal. Needless to say, their tears turned to laughter.

Until the little boy reminded his family of what to do, the culture in the home had overpowered what they had been taught. This family was never the same. Because of this incident, they began to change the culture in their home once and for all.

While this book focuses heavily on the topic of parents creating the culture of their homes, the above story shows us that we can also allow our children to adjust our family's culture when needed. Sometimes they will learn something in church that can cause a shift in the culture of the home. When we make room for them to share and implement the necessary changes, the true culture of our home becomes more like heaven. Regardless of whether the truth that reaches our children comes from us or from our children's pastors, the end result is that they will have that truth solidified by demonstration and experience.

THE NEED FOR EXPERIENCE

As I was brushing my teeth one Saturday night, I heard the Lord say, *Tomorrow, in the first service there will be a child to whom I am giving a dream tonight. The dream is about a duck-billed platypus that is moving in and out of the water.* I stopped brushing my teeth and started taking notes about the dream, the interpretation and the prophetic word the Lord wanted the child to receive from the dream the following morning.

While closing worship the next morning, I asked if any children had experienced a dream the night before about a duck-billed platypus. Sure enough, one girl raised her hand. I told her that God had given her the dream and that I was to tell her what it meant. I could feel the power of God very strongly as I spoke to her. I found out later that her family never attended the first service. On this particular morning, however, she had woken up early and told them she wanted to go. Her parents called her grandmother to see if she could pick her up and bring her to church, which she could. I was wrecked with how God had orchestrated the entire experience.

We had another young man in our church who, because of this example, became hungry to see God work through him in a similar way. It was not long before he came to the stage with a message that God had given him for the kids in the room. Many times, he would close out our worship time with ministry. This young man could lead our time of ministry better than a lot of pastors. It was incredible to watch.

One Sunday, we took several children to the main sanctuary to give them an opportunity to share words of knowledge and to minister healing to the nearly one thousand people in attendance. This young man basically ran the entire ministry time with little help from me.

A few years later he moved with his family back to Switzerland. When I received an invite to speak at a conference in Switzerland, I contacted him and asked if he would like to meet me there. This time there were three thousand people in the adult meetings. As before, he joined me in helping lead the time of ministry, complete with sharing words of knowledge and praying over the sick.

Time and time again I would give the microphone to this young man and let him minister. He demonstrated constantly that there is no such thing as a junior Holy Spirit. At one point in the service, we sent the children from the children's ministry out into the congregation to pray for those who were standing. I will never forget when someone told us afterwards that as a young child ran past him, he was healed instantly in his neck and back. Children can experience the same things that adults experience.

I know that I was not the only one in this young man's life who was encouraging him and giving him opportunity to practice moving in ministry. He has an incredible family who stewarded well everything God was doing with him. They were raising a Spirit-led kid, and our children's ministry team was simply adding fuel to their fire. This young man's life had a major impact on both children and adults. Those who were able to watch him minister saw how important it is to let children experience the Holy Spirit.

The book of Judges shares both the failure of a past generation and a promise for ours.

All that generation also were gathered to their fathers; and there arose another generation after them who did not know the LORD, nor yet the work which He had done for Israel. Then the sons of Israel did evil in the sight of the LORD and served the Baals, and they forsook the LORD, the God of their fathers.

Judges 2:10–12 NASB

This verse is not saying that this generation did not know about God and His works. These were Israelite children—they knew the stories. The failure came from the fact that the families had passed down information but had not created culture. The word *know* in this verse reveals that the children had not encountered God, nor experienced His works for themselves. This serves as a warning for us so that we know what not to repeat. The promise is, however, that if we by demonstration and experience create culture with our children, they will do right in the sight of God, serve Him and refuse to forsake Him.

REFLECTING ON THE EXPERIENCES

Once our children have seen demonstrations of God's power and have had experiences with Him, it is important that they form these into coherent beliefs. The family with the dog not only celebrated the experience they had, but they talked it over and let it reshape what they believed and how they would live from then on. I was able to help the girl who had the dream about the platypus form new beliefs about her relationship with God.

My family was driving home one afternoon when we noticed a man on the corner holding a sign that asked for assistance. We pulled over, gathered the cash that we had on us and walked up to him. We asked his name, what he needed and how he had gotten into his current situation. His story was horrendous. He had family in jail, kids who despised him, disease in his legs and he was struggling to afford his home. We gave him money and asked if he would allow us to pray. He did, and we all laid hands on him and prayed for a couple of minutes. We thanked him and headed back to the car. As we drove away, I asked my children questions so that I could help them articulate what had happened.

My kids expressed that they learned that giving the man a gift opened his heart to receive prayer. I asked my children what they felt for him as we talked. They commented how they felt like they loved him even though they barely knew his name. We discussed that when we minister to people, God allows us to feel the love that He has for them. I asked them if they sensed anything else as we prayed. They could sense tremendous peace and hope, which was us becoming aware of God's perspective of the man's situation. By the time we arrived home, we had formed the experience into a set of words that created beliefs in us as a family.

The entire thing was a beautiful experience for us as parents. "I have more understanding than all my teachers, for your testimonies are my meditation" (Psalm 119:99 ESV). Reflecting on what God has done in our lives is meditating on His testimonies. Doing so gives us understanding as to how His Kingdom operates.

PARENTING LIKE THE FATHER

Demonstration, experience and reflection are three elements we should use when building our home with God. They can be boiled down simply to this one thing: the overflow of our relationship with God. As our relationship with God spills into our children, the culture of our family is influenced. Our connection to Him means we will not build a culture of empty performance, but rather a lifestyle full of God's presence. This is how we build our homes to look and feel like heaven on earth. If there is one thing that I pray for all of us, it is that we truly live as sons and daughters who see our Father for who He is so that our connection with Him translates into our children's connection with Him.

PRAYER PROMPT

Ask the Lord to allow you to experience His goodness and to shift the way you think. Ask God to give your family members a deeper revelation of their identity as sons and daughters who see Him for who He is. Ask Him to help your whole family grow continually and have a deeper connection with Him.

2

THE WAY THEY SHOULD GO

When it comes to parenting, one of the most quoted Bible verses is "Train up a child in the way he should go, and when he is old he will not depart from it" (Proverbs 22:6). Unfortunately, many of us have believed an inaccurate interpretation of this verse. We have understood the verse to read, "Train up our children in all of the ways that they should not go."

If we are focused on all the things our children are not allowed to do, there is no "way" they are to go, and only "ways" to avoid. If we parent from this misinterpretation of the verse, we risk fostering a life of reaction in our children. They will be concerned more about what they are not supposed to do rather than being focused on what their life purpose is. "The way they should go" carries with it a sense of direction. It implies that our children can live with an understanding of the reason they were born. They can know why they were sent to earth.

I think of this in terms of airline tickets. In order to board the correct plane that is heading toward my destination, I am given a ticket that tells me what gate to go find. By directing me only to the gate I am to use, the ticket also tells me to ignore all other gates. If the ticket told me all of the gates my flight would not be at, I could end up wandering frantically all over the airport. Once I know my gate, however, I can walk directly toward it.

This frantic wandering is how many people live their lives. It is not something that we want for our kids. Once our children know "the way they should go," they can look for the signs that will direct them there. In order for us to train our children in the way they should go, we do also need to point out the ways they should not go. Samson is the perfect example of this in the Bible. An angel of the Lord comes to his mother and says:

> "It is true that you are barren and have no children; but you will conceive and give birth to a son. Now please be careful not to drink wine or strong drink, and not to eat anything unclean. For behold, you will conceive and give birth to a son. And no razor shall come over his head, because the boy will be a Nazirite to God from the womb, and he will begin the deliverance of Israel from the hand of the Philistines."
>
> Judges 13:3–5 BSB

The angel told her not to drink wine or strong drink and not to eat anything unclean, nor was she allowed to cut Samson's hair. The angel gave her and her son things they were not allowed to do (the ways they should not go), but finished with the reason why, telling her who he would be and what he was coming to do (the way he should go).

Imagine a young Samson in the middle of summer begging his mom for a haircut. I am sure she had to tell him no at least one thousand times.

Like all children, I am sure that for every time she told him no, he replied with a whine, "Why?" Every time, though, she had an answer straight from God for him.

"You are here to deliver Israel from the hand of the Philistines. By keeping your hair, you will have such strength there will be no enemy who can touch you."

She had to tell him the ways he could not go, but she kept the way he should go in mind. We all know how the story went. Unfortunately, Samson lost sight of the way he was supposed to go, and he had to learn an incredibly difficult lesson. As promised, however, he returned eventually to what he was born to do.

THE IMPORTANCE OF ENCOUNTER

My favorite part of the Samson story is that his mom and dad were both given personal instructions directly from God. The parenting of their son was set on a specific course based off of encounters with God. This was not the only place that this happened in the Bible. The New Testament, for example, begins with Joseph having dreams and angelic visits. During those encounters, he was given specific instructions on how to make decisions within his relationship with Mary, as well as when and where to move his family in order to protect them. Correction, direction and protection came to Joseph every time he needed it. If God did it for these parents, He will do it for us.

Another way to look at this is that we may not find all of the answers regarding the way we are to train our children from the Bible alone. We need personal encounters with God on behalf of our children just as the parents of biblical times did. Our children are equally unique in who they are, and they have unique purposes on earth. God's strategy for one will not be what He has for another.

Both Samson's parents and Samuel's parents received encounters with God for their sons, but each received unique and different instructions. Jesus, who would live His life in perfect obedience to the Father, grew up in a home where his parents demonstrated a lifestyle of obedience. They did whatever

God told them to do. As parents, they would have told Him the stories of their obedience and how it affected them. This taught Him to live the same way. If we parent our children from encounters with God, we will foster in them a lifestyle of encountering Him as well.

When our daughter was born, God said to my wife, *Make sure not to control this one.* That one instruction has helped us time and time again. We have always been intentional to give each of our children lots of freedom to make decisions and experience the consequences, but with her, we know we must be focused especially on this.

One afternoon while we were on the back porch, she picked up a dirty, nasty piece of soft plastic from somewhere and began chewing on it. I started to tell her not to chew on it, but then I remembered what God had said. I backed up and started over, explaining to her that she was welcome to chew on it but that some of the chemicals inside the plastic could cause long-term illness. I then gave her the freedom to make the choice of whether or not she wanted to continue chewing the plastic. Within a few seconds of thinking it through, our six-year-old decided not to chew it and threw it in the garbage.

One brief instruction from God has empowered us to help our daughter to make better decisions on her own.

TRAINING IS MORE THAN EXPLAINING

The Hebrew meaning of the word *train* in Proverbs 22:6 gives us some insight into how we should interpret this verse. The word includes the ideas of "putting something in the mouth," and "to give to be tasted."[1] As parents, we must not only tell our children the way they should go, but we must create op-

1. "Chanak," *Blue Letter Bible*, 2020, https://www.blueletterbible.org/lang/lexicon/lexicon.cfm?Strongs=H2596&t=KJV.

portunities for them to experience it. This is similar to trying to explain what your favorite food tastes like. You can explain it as much as you want, but until your children taste it for themselves, they will not have any idea why it is your favorite or whether or not they will like it.

One area this played out in our family was when our daughter began having painful experiences at school. She hit the age where kids began saying hurtful things to her on the playground. As she explained a specific scenario, she told me that when she was hurt, she shut down and did not know what to do. I started giving her advice about what she could say to her classmates when this happened again. I talked with her about setting boundaries with her friends and communicating to them how what they were doing was affecting her. While I felt as if I was doing a good job explaining how to handle the situation, I could tell my reasoning was not really getting through to her. I was telling her what she could do next time, but I was not training her. I thought I had no way to bring her into the experience of what I was saying.

I aimed my heart to the Lord quickly, and He gave me an idea. I told her to finish my sentences. I went back through the scenarios she had told me had happened earlier that day.

When I got to the part where she had shut down, I said, "He took the ball from you and said, 'You don't get to play with us!' You said . . ." Instantly, she finished my sentence by responding to the boy who had hurt her feelings. I ran through every scenario several times, and each time she finished my sentences. She was practicing what she would do the next time something like this happened. Now I was not explaining, I was training.

In our brains, the more we have experiences or make decisions, the more we create ruts for our thinking and behavior. I imagine that our thoughts are similar to a covered wagon that is directed easily by ruts in the ground. The more we travel on those ruts, the more they guide our journey.

In my daughter's case, the more that she shut down and did not say anything, the deeper the ruts of that behavior became. Because of this, the easier it would be for her to shut down the next time. The more she shut down, the less power she had to do anything else. Her mental options would have become fewer and fewer, and before any of us would have realized what had happened, she would have been struggling to go the way she should.

If I had persisted in simply telling her how to behave differently, I would have succeeded only in pointing her to another path she would have needed to create on her own. When the situation happened again, she would still have faced the challenge of getting out of the old ruts. By having her practice and finish my sentences, I led her down a new path and helped her create new ruts. That way when she found herself in a similar situation again it would be easier for her to take the new path.

WHAT WE ALLOW IN

Not only do we invite our children into a lifestyle of encounters with God by modeling our own encounters with Him, but we can model other things as well—some of which may be things we do not want present in our families.

There is a church I visit whose pastor has two adult children, both of whom I respect highly. Every time I am with this pastor, I ask him for some wisdom that he has acquired from his years of parenting. During one conversation, he told me how his son had always been a very grateful child. Out of nowhere, however, he started acting entitled and ungrateful. Before he did anything else, this dad went to prayer. When he did that, the Lord showed him that he, the father, had allowed ungratefulness into his own life. In turn, this had seeped into his son's life.

Rather than correct his son for being ungrateful, the Lord told him to apologize to his son for allowing ungratefulness into his own life. After all, the son (like all kids) had simply been doing what he had seen his father do. The father took his son out for a treat and apologized to him for what he had let into his life. He then asked his son to forgive him. The son forgave him, and from that point on he was grateful again.

Charles Spurgeon, who was a highly influential British pastor, said, "Train up a child in the way he should go—but be sure you go that way yourself."[2]

THE PARENTING PRAYER

My favorite parenting prayer in the Bible is from the story of Samson we discussed earlier (see Judges 13). Samson's mother had experienced an angelic visit during which the angel told her that she would have a child, even though she had been barren previously. The angel gave her specific instructions about her diet and how to raise her future son. Manoah, however, missed this encounter and the instructions his wife had received. In response, he prayed this prayer: "O my Lord, please let the Man of God whom You sent come to us again and teach us what we shall do for the child who will be born" (Judges 13:8).

God listened to his prayer, and the angel came again. Manoah got to hear the instructions firsthand. The reason this is my favorite parenting prayer is because I can relate with Manoah's desire to have specific and clear leadership from God in the lives of my children. We are able to see in Scripture how this encounter had a profound impact on Samson's life, and I am able to see through my own life how these kinds of encounters have profoundly guided my own family's life. Because of this, I pray this type of prayer on a regular basis.

2. Charles Spurgeon, "Spurgeon Quotes," *Prince of Preachers*, Sept. 21, 2017, https://www.princeofpreachers.org/quotes/train-up-a-child-in-the-way-he-should-go.

PRAYER PROMPT

Has God already spoken to you directly about one of your children? If so, list a few of those words out. What advice or instruction did He give you?

Ask the Lord for help addressing a specific situation you are facing with your children right now. Ask Him to teach you what to do. Ask for His wisdom and insight into who your children are to be and the way they should go. Write down any new words or directions that He gives you.

3

STAY A NOVICE

WE DO NOT KNOW WHAT WE ARE DOING

When I was a children's pastor at Bethel, people would travel from all over the world to learn from us about how to do children's ministry better. Oftentimes I would open our conferences by telling everyone, "We have no idea what we are doing."

I would wait a few seconds to let that statement sink in. The audiences were comprised of people who had traveled from all over and had given a week of their lives to learn about how to improve upon their children's ministry. In spite of that, we had just declared that we did not know what we were doing.

I would then explain that I was not telling them we were clueless; rather, I was revealing to them our greatest strength as a team. We made sure that no matter what was going right, we would never allow ourselves to come to the place where we thought that we were experts. We worked hard to remain in the place of a novice who is dependent fully on God for His help and direction.

As we begin this chapter, I want to tell you the same thing. Our greatest strength as parents will be to remain humble and teachable. We should not get to the point where we believe that we know what we are doing. I do not, of course, mean that we refuse to learn, grow or become more confident in our parenting; instead, we should stay connected to the one who knows exactly what He is doing. We need to remain in the posture of a novice. We do not ever want to get to a place where we think we know exactly what to do, and we do not want to put ourselves in a position where we no longer depend on the Father for His help.

We all have experienced those times as parents where something changes as soon as we think we have it all figured out. We then realize how little we know. We should remain dependent on God for His input intentionally. If we do ever get to the place where we are no longer dependent on Him and we think we can do this on our own, then we have fallen for the same trick that Eve fell for in the garden.

AFRAID TO FATHER A SON

My second child, August, was my first son. When he was born, I had two of the most horrendous days of my life. We had been awake all night long with his delivery, and when his big sister woke up the next morning, she began throwing up. We knew that it would be really bad if he caught whatever sickness she had, and we were really afraid. Because of a lack of sleep and fear of our day-old son getting very sick, I became snippy with everyone in our house. For an entire day I was rude to both my mother-in-law and my wife. It got to the point where Lauren told me I needed to leave the house, seek God and figure out what my problem was. She told me not to come back until I was ready to be fun to be around.

I left the house with my journal and went to a nearby park. I sat down and wrote out everything from my perspective that was going on. I wrote to God that I was afraid my son was going to die. All of a sudden, He spoke to my heart: *That is not the real problem.*

He continued to explain to me that when my daughter was born, I was in uncharted territory. Because I am one of those people who do pretty well with the unknown, I get excited for the adventure. When I do not know what is coming, I take it as a challenge. To me, therefore, having a daughter was a brand-new adventure. God pointed out to me that with my son it was different. This was not uncharted territory for me. Not only did I have a little experience with parenting, I also had experience with the father-son relationship. I grew up in a home with divorced parents, and what I knew about fathers and sons was that fathers are not there for their boys.

He then went on to reveal to me that while I had been excited to be a dad to a daughter, I was afraid to be a dad to a son. His words rang true to me, and I told Him that He was right (of course He was)—I had been afraid, and I had no idea what I was doing. His reply was, *Good. That is exactly where I want you to be.* The people who think that they know what they are doing often end up cutting themselves off from their need for God.

Later that day when I got home, I apologized to everyone, including my son. One-day-old babies do not understand apologies with their minds, but I was not speaking to his mind, but to his heart. I told him I had been afraid because I had not been able to see how a dad functions or ministers in the home. I admitted that I did not know what I was doing. I told him I would learn from other fathers, but above all I promised him that I would learn from Father God and would do my best. With His help, I was no longer afraid. I finished by telling him that I would be present. From that moment on I have not been afraid, and I have loved having sons.

All of us have moments as parents where we realize that we do not know what we are doing. Too often we go to the internet or to books for help. Books and the advice of other parents can be of great help, of course, but they are not the best source for truth. When we reach out to the wisdom of our peers, we are reaching out to other "contractors." When we reach out to God, we are getting advice from the "Architect." He is the only one who knows the specifics of each individual child and what we need to raise them.

BUY THAT BOY SOME THROWING KNIVES

My father-in-law has three daughters, and now that they are all married, he has three sons-in-law. Since his daughters never enjoyed hunting, one of his favorite things to do with us is to take us hunting. One year, we were all going on a week-long elk hunting trip in New Mexico. There were 13,000 acres of wild land that we were going to roam to look for elk. For us young men, this was a first. We had hunted ducks together before but never elk. This was another level.

I had everything in place, had taken hours of hunter safety courses and was ready to go—or so I thought. The plan was that I would join the rest of them in New Mexico after I completed another trip that I had scheduled. A couple of days before I was to join them, I realized that I had not gotten my hunting license for the state of New Mexico. I tried everything I could to figure out how to get a license last minute before I arrived in New Mexico, but nothing was working. I know it may not seem like a big deal to most people, but it was to me. I ended up quickly in a bad place emotionally.

I started questioning whether or not hunting was something I wanted to do. I began questioning my manhood, and I asked myself questions like, "Did I sabotage this trip subconsciously so that I could not go because deep inside I am not this type of man?" (I am not saying that hunting and killing animals is the only thing that makes a real man, but at this point in my life, the hunting trip was my attempt to connect with part of my identity as a man.)

I felt the Lord invite me to come talk to Him. I closed my eyes and pictured the Father. Immediately, He reminded me of a scenario when I was a young boy. I had purchased some throwing knives with my allowance money. I got in a lot of trouble, because I was trying to throw them at everything. The Father reminded me that I am the type of man who enjoys hunting, but somewhere between childhood and now I had lost that aspect of myself. He showed me that this trip was going to reawaken something that had been in me all along. He also told me not to worry about the license.

Before I opened my eyes, God showed me a picture of my son, and He told me to buy him throwing knives for Christmas. He was five at the time. Yes, Jesus told me to buy my five-year-old son throwing knives. Not only did I not know how to be a father to a son, I began to wonder if God knew!

When I got to New Mexico, my father-in-law already had a license for me. I had allowed myself to get all worked up and stressed out for nothing. I then got online and ordered my son twelve throwing knives and a nice case.

When the week-long hunting trip came to an end, we each went home with the meat from our own elks. Hunting elk in the wild was an incredible experience, and it reawakened something inside me. I woke up long before the sun, prepared for and braved the elements, waited patiently, remained calm under pressure and provided a year's worth of nourishment for my family. I did not just go to the store to get meat, I went out onto 13,000 acres and got it for us. I was that type of man—but I had not seen it until then.

The process of hunting also connected with me on a deep, spiritual level. I had chosen to take an elk's life, and it would now nourish and sustain my entire family and many friends. This was similar to how my choices took the Lamb of God's life. He now sustains and nourishes me. The gratitude that I felt toward the elk for giving its life to sustain others was similar to (but nowhere near as much) the gratitude I have for Jesus.

A couple of months later we celebrated Christmas. I could not wait to give my son his gift. On Christmas Eve, I took him outside to cut some wood with me. He asked why we were doing this, and I told him he would find out tomorrow as it was part of his gift.

The next morning arrived, and he opened every other gift first. We finally got to the knives. When he unzipped the case and realized what was inside, he jumped on me and hugged me unlike any other hug he had given me before. I had given my son a gift that was not only something he would play with for years to come, but I had called him out as a young man. From all of our previous conversations he and I had had about knives, my son knew that his freedom to use them was dependent on his demonstration that he could be trusted with them. When he saw the knives, he knew that he had shown me that I could trust him with them.

The knives were much more than a cool gift. They were the recognition that he had been consistently safe in his handling of dangerous things. As he unzipped the case to see what was inside, it was as if he got a glimpse of what was truly in his heart. The knives had a deep impact on both of us. I enjoyed the moment and the hug, but more than that I was overwhelmed with how God knew exactly how to help me father my son. Five years earlier I had been afraid to be his dad, but with God's direction, I now looked like I knew what I was doing.

BUILDING TRUST

I know it sounds crazy to give a five-year-old boy throwing knives, but he is now seven years old and has eighteen throwing knives, several pocketknives, three hatchets and one machete, totaling more than forty blades. With the exception of the pocketknives, he throws each of these at the target we made together.

When he got his first knife at three years old, I took the time to explain to him that his freedom to have and use knives would be determined by how much trust he had built with them. If he used them correctly, and only when he was with me, he would increase my trust in him and would get to use them more. Only once has he broken a bit of trust and had to lose some privileges. Even in that situation, when I gave him a chance to rebuild the trust, he did.

He begged me nearly every day to use his tiny Swiss Army knife. As often as we could, we would sit down and whittle on some wood. I held his hand as we cut away from ourselves. I showed him how the blade did not lock and could cut him easily if it closed. Learning this on a folding knife with no lock (the most dangerous kind) was beneficial. He knew he had to be extra careful or that blade would close on his fingers.

Over and over again as he remained focused and careful, he built more trust with me. I made sure to let him know that. There were many times I had to tell him no because I did not have the time right then to sit and use the knife with him. In those moments we discussed how his tone of voice and attitude about my no also affected my ability to trust his level of maturity in being able to handle knives. If he could not handle my *no* when it was necessary, I could not be confident he could handle a blade when I said yes.

One time he was walking with his throwing knives away from the target and back to his throwing line when he tripped on a sprinkler and fell. He held the knives out and hit the ground with his body, not using his hands at all to catch his fall. I picked him up quickly as he began to cry. I held him, and we talked it through.

I was scared that he had hurt himself, but that was not his concern. He was really only afraid that he had broken my trust when he fell. I assured him that he had not broken any trust, as the fall was a simple mistake. I assured him that the way he had handled the fall actually built trust with me. He had demonstrated that he could handle the knives even then. I wiped his tears, and we went right back to throwing.

The knives were kept out of his reach. One day, however, he learned how to get to them without my help. I saw him holding one of his knives, and I gently took it from him. I told him that the choice he had made to get his knife without permission had damaged some of the trust he had been building and that he would not be able to use his knife at all for a week or so.

He was devastated, and I held him as he cried. I told him that even though he had damaged trust I would give him a chance to rebuild it. I asked if he wanted that. He did, of course, and when the week was over, I got out his knife and invited him to come cut some wood with it. As we began to cut, I reminded him that this time and the next few times with his knife would either rebuild my trust or damage it even more. He was more careful than ever, and he rebuilt not only what trust he had damaged, but much more.

The knives have been a practical tool to teach August some of the most valuable lessons about life. When we talk about friends, ladders, cars or guns, I refer to the knives and trust levels. If he wants freedom to drive, he knows it is all dependent on trust. If he wants to be a good friend, he knows it is also about trust.

What he has learned from knives influences many other areas of his life. This one thing has made him one of the most trustworthy people I know (and he is still only seven years old). I only need to say the words "trust level" and he steps right up and shows what he is capable of. I tell you, the money I spent on those blades has brought something priceless into our home. The Father knew how to help me when I not only had no clue what I was doing, but when I was also in the middle of my own crisis of identity.

I help lead a father/son camp every year, and when he was six years old, he brought one of his knives to camp. We overheard another boy who was older than August asking his dad why he did not have his own knife yet like August did. The dad replied that he could not yet trust his son with his own knife. When August heard this, he looked at me with the widest eyes I have ever seen. He realized how important trust is, and he saw how much trust he had built. I winked and nodded in his direction.

Not only did God use throwing knives to remind me who I am, He also continues to use them to help me develop August into the man he will become. Through those knives my son and I both have learned the value of building trust by doing things the way God tells us.

ASK THE FATHER

I have a friend who has an incredible inner healing ministry. She meets with people from all over the world and from all walks of life, from the poor to celebrities. She has a gift to be able to see past situations and directly to the roots of people's issues. Because of that ability people can become dependent on her. She works really hard to make sure they do not become dependent by always directing them to ask God about their situations.

Many people call her and ask her what God is saying. It frustrates her so much that she created her email address to include the phrase "ask the Lord." She tells people quite often that if they would spend as much time seeking God as they do asking others for advice they would not need as much advice. With these words she is trying to reveal to people how often we tend to go to everyone else but God. This approach is similar to what pastor Bill Johnson does. When people ask him for advice, he rarely gives any. Most often he asks the person, "What is God saying to you?"

In John 16, Jesus teaches something significant about prayer. He redirects where His disciples should aim their questions and requests. "And in that day you will ask Me nothing. Most assuredly, I say to you, whatever you ask the Father in My name He will give you" (John 16:23). Jesus is not saying that you cannot talk to Him when you pray; rather, He is saying that He gave us His access to the Father. The same Father who taught Him all things will also teach us (see John 8:28). In this context, Jesus sums up what He has been doing all along. He gives His disciples their own relationship with the Father, which is the same relationship that He has with His Father. This is the access we now have as parents. We can go directly to "The Parent."

What does this mean for us and for what we are to do with our children? We are not only to demonstrate our relationship with God to them, but we are also to encourage them to have their own relationship with Him. At some point our children need their relationship with God to become their own and not just based off ours.

This frees us to remain novices as parents. I do not need to have every answer for every situation that comes up. I can direct my kids to Him. I tell them that instead of asking me when they have questions, they can ask God. We ask them questions like, "What is God showing you about this?" or "Have you asked God what He thinks?" If they do not know or have not asked Him already, we lead them. Each time we do, we are training them to go to Him for help as Jesus did with the disciples. Again, if I am demonstrating a life in which I go to God for His input, it is much easier to lead my children into that same lifestyle.

BEACH HOUSE FOR A MONTH

A few years back, I was speaking at a church in the Washington, D.C., area. God had given one of the pastors a picture for me, and he asked if he could tell me. I said yes, of course, because

I always want to know what God is showing me or saying to me, especially if He is showing it to someone else.

The pastor began by saying that he had seen a picture of my family living in a beach house for thirty days. I was excited, but quickly realized that unless God gave us a massive miracle, a week-long beach vacation would not be feasible. The pastor continued and said that over the door of the beach house were the words "No WIFI."

I heard the Lord whisper to me that if I went thirty days without WIFI, my own house could feel like a beach house. I decided right then that as soon as I got home from the trip, I would not use the internet while I was with my family. As I drove into the driveway of my home in the evenings, I pulled out my phone and turned off the signal. I started calling the airplane mode feature on my phone "family mode."

I immediately began to notice a few things. I realized that whenever I did not know what to do, I would try to avoid the entire situation by going to my phone. I even caught my hand going toward my phone automatically whenever I felt a slight bit uncomfortable (a sign of addiction). Without the internet, I could no longer do this. Instead of going to my phone to avoid a tough situation, I began going to God to engage Him about it. I was going to Him for help instead of going to my phone for distraction.

During this time, I saw an image of a child who was sitting at the dinner table with both parents who were on their phones. The caption said, "I wish I was their phone so that they would hold me and look at me all day." This motivated me even more to become more present with God and to be more present with my kids.

I discovered through experience that God is our "ever-present help in trouble" (Psalm 46:1 NIV). My access to Him was not just a theory but a reality. I also started expressing more of God's nature to my wife and children as I became ever-present instead of sometimes present. I became more concerned about being an active participant in my story rather than posting pictures to my Instagram story. It is sad to admit this, but my children no longer needed to call out to me multiple times before they got my attention.

I heard God ask me, *How would you live if your family was the subject of a reality TV show and cameras were recording everything?* That question helped me realize that there are tiny cameras (my children's eyes) in my home not only recording everything, but also playing it back to me unedited.

Since I was not using social media, I no longer had to sift through other people's opinions in order to find out what God was saying. That alone was worth the entire thirty-day journey. The inspiration God was sending me no longer needed to cut through the other mass quantities of information I was receiving.

While we did not live anywhere near the beach, I began noticing more and more how beautiful my city was, and every day ended with my being disconnected from work as if I were at a real beach house.

It happened. I had a thirty-day vacation that came in daily chunks, and all I did was turn off my internet. By doing so, I had returned to the place of being a novice.

THE NOVICE

Remaining a novice is another way of saying we do not ever want to leave the realm of simple trust in our Father. It is not checking out and resigning to "I have no idea what I'm doing." Rather, it is going to Him because He knows what He is doing. It prevents us from getting to a place where we are raising our children based on principles alone or on what the latest child psychologist or "expert" says to do. These things are helpful, for sure, and many things are common during certain ages. But at the same time, each child is unique, and only God knows exactly what children need and how to give it to them.

Every time we ask God what He thinks and what He is saying, we are trusting His guidance instead of our own understanding (see Proverbs 3:5–6). And we are building the same thing inside of our children. When we do not know what to do, He does. We have access to Him. We have the same access Jesus has. Why would we want to ever be limited to our own expertise or understanding?

PRAYER PROMPT

Ask Jesus to help you to rely on Him continuously instead of asking others for advice or filtering your decisions through others' opinions. Ask Him for divine wisdom and direction, and ask Him to show you what to do and how to do it.

Ask Him to reveal to you if there has been any kind of disconnection with Him or your family, and ask Him for the grace to engage even in the tough situations.

PART 2

THE
SPIRIT-GUIDED
PARENT

4

RAISING SONS
AND DAUGHTERS

The book of Luke contains some incredible counsel for us as we seek to create true culture in our homes. It is the story known commonly as the Prodigal Son (see Luke 15). The narrative is about more than the younger son's poor choices. It is also about the older son's good choices that were motivated by a bad belief system. And ultimately, it is about how the father adjusted his sons' inaccurate understanding of his character.

As we know, this story is a picture of the home that God creates. Both sons have grown up with this father, who represents Father God, the only perfect father, and yet neither one of them can see it. Based on their choices, it is obvious that they have no idea who their father is. They grow up in the perfect home but live as if they are orphans. Children who have no home are not the only ones who can be influenced by the orphan spirit. The orphan spirit gains influence when we agree with any of the devil's lies—but more specifically, the lie of believing that we do not have a good Father who will take care of us. When we believe a lie such as this, we begin to live in a way that is inconsistent with who we truly are.

Both boys had an orphan mindset, and their father was willing to do what was necessary to remove it. He wanted sons, not orphans, living in his home.

The older son in the story was living like a slave who worked hard in the fields and never disobeyed (see Luke 15:29). He reminded his dad angrily that he had been serving him for many years. The word *serving* that he used can mean "to be a slave," but it can also mean "to yield obedience." His accusation toward his father was as if he said, "I yielded obedience to your requests. I have never done anything else my entire life. I have lived for years as if I were a slave, and you have never once done for me what you have done for my brother who left!"

Please keep in mind here that serving and obeying God does not make a person a slave or an orphan automatically, as these positions can be held even by sons. This brother's anger and lack of enjoyment of his father's abundance, however, shows us that he had been serving and obeying his father with the mindset of a slave.

The younger son in the story did not want to live the way his older brother had been living, so he asked for his inheritance early. In doing so, he treated his father as if he were already dead. We read that the father gave his younger son the inheritance that he requested even though he knew his son would not do well with it. He allowed him the freedom to leave and make terrible choices in the hope that his son would realize what he had in his own home. We often do not realize what we have until we have walked away from it.

This is the beginning of the process of removing the orphan mindset from this son. When the younger son realizes what he had and remembers who he is, he heads home. As soon as the father sees his son, he runs toward him. After receiving hugs and kisses from his dad, the young man begins to confess what he has done. This is where it gets interesting.

The father interrupts his son mid-confession and seems to ignore his son's request to become an employee. Why? So that the father can start a party. The process of interrupting, ignoring and party-starting is how he chose to remove the orphan mindset.

When the younger son was in the pigpen and discovered what he had left behind, the Bible says he "came to himself" (Luke 15:17). In other words, not only did he not know his father's character, but he also had forgotten who he was. As he looked at and contemplated eating the pods that the pigs were fed, he began to remember who he was.

This is where we see clearly the difference between repentance and confession. Many believers think they are the same, but they are not. Thinking that they are the same is what causes many to continue living sinful lives even after they have repented.

We have all had times in our lives when we confessed our sins but continued to do the same things. Many marriages have ended because of this process. Confession is important and can help us get to the place of repentance; however, confession is only acknowledging what we have done. Repentance, on the other hand, is discovering why we did it and turning from what caused us to sin.

We confess and then ask ourselves, "How did I get to this place?" or "What belief caused me to do that?" When we can answer those questions, we can then repent with the hope that we will no longer repeat the behavior to which we have confessed.

In the story of the Prodigal Son, the father ignores his son's confession as if it is of no interest to him. He seems to be interested only in the party. Why?

Because his son is attempting to lower his identity to that of a slave and wants his father to become his boss. The reason the father both ignores and interrupts his son's confession is because he's solidifying his son's repentance. He wasn't interested in confession alone, but true repentance.

There was no need for the son to continue to offer himself as a hired servant. When the son came to himself while still in the pigpen, his repentance had begun. The pigpen allowed him to see that he had been living as someone he was not. The father knew that the final step of repentance was not his son merely admitting what he had done and coming back to the house as a slave, but for the boy to return to his true identity as a son.

Imagine with me what was running through the father's mind as his son tried to explain why he had returned. He might have been thinking, "You cannot change who you are to me by making poor choices. Those poor choices do not control my opinion of you. They are, however, attempting to control your thoughts about who you are, so I will interrupt you and tell you the truth. You are trying to humiliate yourself, and I will have none of it. I want humility, and the way I give it back to you is to get this party started and finally show you who you have been all along."

The entire interaction between the father and his younger son demonstrates the tendency our children have to connect what they have done wrong with how we will think of them. It warns us to handle their mistakes and sins carefully. If we do not bring our children to full restoration of relationship, we can inadvertently instill the orphan mindset into them.

The orphan mindset is instilled whenever shame is allowed to remain. Shame attempts to visit our children often, and when it does, it calls them names based on what they have done. It also invites us to give them that same identity. The word *accuser* that is used of the devil (see Revelation 12:10) is the Greek word *kategoros*, which is where we get our word *category*. The devil wants to categorize our children based on their sins instead of their positions as sons and daughters, which is the only category in which God puts them.

And not only does the devil want to categorize them that way, he wants us to help him. If he succeeds, our children will struggle with that sin for as long as they believe it is their identity. People always live out who they believe they are. It is easy for a child who has lied to think of themselves as a liar. It is also far too common for parents to call their children liars and to treat them as if that is who they are. When parents do this, they can only attempt to manage their children's behavior instead of being able to allow their children's true identity to express itself through their behavior. If this happens, parents are left only with the option of trying to control their children.

Too often we attempt to control our children by trying to prevent them from making poor choices. If we do not allow children the freedom to make poor choices, they also are not allowed to make good ones. By our control over them, we risk removing their ability to make their own choices altogether. Both of the sons in our story fell into this trap. When it came to his father, the younger son confessed not only his sin, but he tried to confess what he thought his father wanted: to control him.

He was saying, "Dad, if you let me back on the property, I will let you tell me what to do the rest of my life." This is not at all what the father wanted. He did not want control. He wanted connection. He did not want to tell his son what to do or to manage his behavior. He wanted his son to rediscover who he was and to behave accordingly. In order to remove the influence of the orphan mindset, the father showed his son the truth about them both. The father would not allow his son to lower his identity to be what he could do for his dad. He would not allow his son's poor choices to determine who he would be.

When the older son heard about the party, he got upset and did not join them. Again, what the father does is incredible. He goes to his older son and invites him personally to come join them. He then allows his boy to explain why he will not go in. The son explains how he has made good choices and served his father all his life. "'My son,' the father said, 'you are always with me, and everything I have is yours'" (Luke 15:31 NIV).

When the father finishes his thought, the story ends. It does not say what happened next. I am sure, however, that the father walked back and joined the party, leaving his older son with the choice to join or stay. The son could either step into sonship or stay in the orphan mindset. In essence, the father attempted to show this son that he did not realize the type of father he had or the kind of home he lived in. The father attempted to remove the orphan mindset with each word that he spoke.

THE ORPHANAGE IN THE MIND

These two sons were not the first people to agree with orphan-type thoughts. These types of lies were introduced to mankind long before Jesus told this story. When it comes to the way we think about the devil, we are often quick to quote the verse that says, "When he [the devil] lies, he speaks out of his own character, for he is a liar and the father of lies" (John 8:44 ESV). Unfortunately, we can look at this verse and assume that the only way the devil operates is by telling lies. When we read his interactions with both Eve and Jesus, we see that he does not always come right out and lie to people. He submits his lies in the form of questions. He invites people to question who God is and the truth about what He has spoken to them.

When the devil approached Eve, he asked her a question that caused her to wonder if God was really as good as He seemed (see Genesis 3:1). She partnered her thinking with his and found herself in agreement with the orphan himself. He tried the same thing with Jesus when he asked Him to perform a miracle in order to prove He was the beloved Son of God (see Matthew 4:1–10). This is the first of two miracles Jesus refused to perform, because sons do not perform for their identity or for love. If Jesus had performed the miracle in an attempt to get love or to demonstrate that He was a son, He would have stepped into the same orphan thinking everyone else on earth was already partnered with.

Many believers my age, myself included, grew up thinking that we had to perform in order to receive love and identity. This has been a challenge for many of us. We have thought that if we behave, then we become. If I tell the truth, for example, I am a truthful person and my parents will love me. If I tell a lie, I am a liar and my parents will not love me.

This belief has created believers whose identities are unstable and confused. I lied yesterday, so I am a liar. I told the truth today, so now I am truthful. This is not how God operates. He calls us truthful and gives us the faith that we are, indeed, truthful. This leads us to tell the truth.

As parents, we must understand this reality. We must, like God, refuse to make our children perform for our love and identity. Our children should not be able to do anything that would cause us not to love them or that would cause their identity to change in our eyes. The father in our story did not control his sons; instead, he allowed them to make choices, even if those choices were poor. He did not demonstrate how good a father he was by the poor choices he prevented, but rather by how he responded when those poor choices were made.

One place this is revealed in our lives is how we treat our young kids in the grocery store. We want them to behave, to be quiet, to sit still or to ride calmly in the cart. For many parents, their goal is to prevent their kids from climbing out, grabbing things or making noise because they are concerned about what other people will think of them. They quickly enter the land of control by trying to prevent their kids from misbehaving, because they think that their kids' obedience will make them look like good parents.

It is important to remember that our children's behavior does not reveal whether we are good parents or not—*our* behavior does. Many children who behave perfectly do so because they have parents who are controlling their behavior. "Do what I told you, because I said so," is a completely different way of parenting than what we saw in the story of the two boys. The father allowed his son to leave and make the decisions he made. He did not chase him down. He let his son learn from the consequences of his choices, which he could only do by not controlling his son. This created a place where his son would learn to think for himself instead of allowing his father to do the thinking for him. It also created a place where the son learned the reasons why obedience is important, as opposed to just hearing "because I said so."

What the father did in the story is similar to what God did with Adam and Eve. He allowed them to do the very thing He told them not to do. Not only did He let them, but He placed the tree in the garden and let the serpent approach Eve. Why? Because He was not going to control them. If He had been a controlling Father, He would have put that tree on the other side of the planet and placed brick walls around it. He would have put the serpent somewhere else altogether.

If we do not understand this, even teaching our children to work with God can become unhealthy. After all, it is always a challenge to work with God when in agreement with another spirit. I have seen many families who use control and fear to get their children to pray, to read their Bibles or to minister to someone else. They do not realize that their attempt to get their kids connected to God is motivated by another spirit entirely. I had a parent tell me that fear works well in getting children to do things we want them to do. I replied, "Sure it works. It is just not how God does things."

I have had times where my children have been adamant that they did not want me to read the Bible to them, specifically when my daughter was seven and my son was five. At this point, I felt like the Holy Spirit told me to go along with their request. For a couple of months, I did not read the Bible to them, and I did not force them to read the Bible when they really did not want to. I still gave them God's Word by sharing with them verses that I had read recently, or I pointed out how a situation in our lives was similar to one from the Bible, but I did not control them by usurping their wishes.

There have been times recently, however, when I have noticed that my daughter's light is on long after she was supposed to have gone to bed. When I have peeked into her room, she has been reading her Bible. On other occasions I have gone into her room to ask what she would like for breakfast to find that she is reading her Bible. She loves it. Why? Because I did not control her.

I am not saying that we should never read the Bible to our kids if they do not want us to. Sometimes it is important to press in and do the things we do not want to do. It is just as important, however, that we do those things without control in our hearts. On the outside, these situations often look similar, if not exactly the same. The way to really tell the difference is by examining our hearts. We have to discern the difference. If there is any hint of anxiety in asking them to do something they do not want to, that is a good sign we may be trying to control them rather than pressing into what is uncomfortable.

In my opinion, Hebrews 5:8 is one of the strangest verses in the Bible. "He learned obedience by the things which He suffered." That seems weird to me, because Jesus never sinned. He never disobeyed His Father. Never. So how could He learn obedience by suffering? I do not know. I do know, though, that this verse does not say Jesus learned obedience by His Father forcing Him to obey.

Allowing our children to experience consequences for disobedience, which is learning why it is important to obey, is possible only if we allow them to disobey. If they can learn this in the safety of our homes when the consequences are along the lines of missing out on a TV show, losing time to play video games or scooping up the dog's poop, it will be easier for them to obey us later when the stakes are higher, such as when we tell them not to do drugs or to choose friends wisely. They will know that listening to their parents is good for them, because they learned obedience the same way Jesus did.

By allowing our children to disobey and receive the consequences of disobedience, we are disciplining them instead of punishing them. Punishment should not be present in our homes. "There is no fear in love; but perfect love casts out fear, because fear involves punishment, and the one who fears is not perfected in love" (1 John 4:18 NASB). We know that if punishment is present, love is not.

This does not mean, however, that we do not discipline our children. "But if you are without chastening, of which all have become partakers, then you are illegitimate and not sons" (Hebrews 12:8). If we do not discipline our children, the Bible says that they are illegitimate. This word is translated as *bastards* in the King James Version, which means "to be without parents." This is another way to say that if we do not discipline our children, we are inviting the orphan spirit to influence their lives.

I have seen many parents who know that punishing their children and using fear is not God's way, but in order to avoid that they end up not disciplining their kids at all. They tell their children not to do something, such as throwing toys at their siblings, but then do not give a consequence when the toy is thrown and the sibling is injured. They, instead, repeat over and over what their child is not supposed to do.

Children, however, do not learn from repeated requests—they learn by experiencing consequences. Maybe the child does not get to go to his friend's house because he threw the toy. That is him suffering. That is him learning that if he throws toys, he cannot play with his friends. It leads him toward the thought, "Maybe I don't want to throw toys anymore because I really want to play with my friends."

The punishment side of this is just as bad. I remember talking with a dad who said that if his son yells at his mom, he makes the son stand in the corner for twenty minutes. Discipline would have the boy sit in a chair until he is ready to talk to his mother in a calm voice. The boy would be free to come out of the chair whenever he has a change of heart that also changes his behavior. If you yell, you sit in the chair. When you are ready not to yell, you can come out. Consequence and discipline.

Standing in the corner for twenty minutes, however, is not discipline. It is punishment. In the punishment scenario, if the boy has a change of heart after one minute of standing in the corner and is now ready to change his behavior, he still has to stand there for another nineteen minutes. He is not learning to be in control of himself. He is learning, instead, that his father is in control of him.

Usually this type of treatment is accompanied by "Stand there and think about what you did!" After the nineteen minutes of punishment are completed and his dad asks him why he yelled at his mom, the son would have to say (if he was given the freedom to be honest), "I was mad, and no one has taught me any other skills." He may even say something like, "Well dad, I was mad, and you yell at me when you are mad so that is what I have learned to do." The boy would never say that, of course, because it would only cause more punishment. Instead of learning to obey, the son learns to hide and to self-protect. That puts the son in the position of protecting himself from the one who should have been protecting him.

God was not punishing Adam and Eve when He enforced the consequence of their having to leave the garden. He was protecting them. God put them out of the garden so they could not eat from the tree of life and live forever in a sinful state (see Genesis 3:22). That is discipline at its finest. He gave consequences that were motivated only by the future well-being of His children.

In contrast, the boy who was punished for yelling at his mom may not yell at his mom anymore, but at some point, that pent up anger will come out. A whole lot can happen in a boy's heart during those nineteen minutes of punishment.

He may end up saying things to himself like, *I will never do this to my kids*, or *My dad hates me*. These are inner vows that set the boy up for a life of misery. Inner vows are those statements we make internally, and sometimes out loud, that cause us to live in reaction to something we do not want to do. They are agreements we make that allow us to be controlled by the trauma we are hoping to avoid.

Once the boy who has made those inner vows grows up, gets married, has kids and his kids disobey, he typically does one of two things. The first is that he does nothing about his child's disobedience because he swore that he would never behave like his dad. That might sound like, *Why are my kids not learning? After all, I am not doing what my father did to me*. The second is that he ends up repeating the exact behavior his father modeled to him but cannot figure out why. He might think to himself, *Why do I hear my father coming out of my mouth when I swore that I would never act like him?*

Both of these outcomes are the result of the orphan mindset. "I hid from my dad because he punished me, and that forced me to figure out life all on my own. I did not ask for help or get my dad's input about my choices because I did not want him to control me. I put up invisible walls, and even though I lived at home with my parents, I raised myself."

Discipline locks the orphan spirit out of our homes. Discipline protects our children's futures. Discipline creates children who grow the fruit of self-control. Discipline leads our children to move through confession and into true repentance. Discipline does what punishment never could—it raises children who live as sons and daughters. Punishment only raises orphans who are fearful of their fathers, who live their lives in hiding and who end up being led by the orphan spirit.

Discipline raises children who can be led by the Spirit of God because they learn from consequences instead of control.

PRAYER PROMPT

Thank Father God for being a good and loving Father who does not try to control you. Ask Him for the grace necessary to love your children through healthy discipline and consequences. Ask Him to help you give them the freedom to learn in a safe environment. Ask Him to reveal to you if you have made any inner vows that are having an effect on your parenting.

5

DREAMING WITH GOD

We all have both negative and positive things that have been passed down to us from our parents, who also had things passed down to them. Some people call these negative things generational curses while others call them generational lies. Whatever term you want to use, we see from the story of Jacob and Laban (see Genesis 30) that we can choose what we receive from those who have come before us.

Jacob had been living with and working for his father-in-law Laban, but he was ready to leave and take his family to a place of their own. Laban did not want him to stop keeping his flocks, because he knew that he had prospered and had been blessed because of Jacob. Laban made Jacob an offer he could not refuse. He said to Jacob, "Name me your wages, and I will give it" (Genesis 30:28). Jacob told Laban that he wanted all of the spotted and speckled sheep for himself, and the rest would be for Laban. Laban agreed, but then he took away all the sheep that were spotted and speckled, thinking that he could manipulate the situation to keep Jacob's flock from growing. But Jacob caused the exact opposite to happen.

Jacob took some rods and cut streaks and spots in them. He placed them in the water troughs where the flocks came to drink. The sheep that were not spotted and speckled started reproducing spotted and speckled lambs. These sheep stopped reproducing according to what had been passed down from previous generations and, instead, reproduced what they were seeing. Jesus is our Shepherd and we are His sheep. He can change what we reproduce in our lives by changing what we are focused on.

We can repeat the pain that we carry from our past into our children's lives if we spend time telling ourselves not to do that exact thing. In other words, by focusing on what our parents did to us, even if our motivation is to avoid doing the same thing, we are in danger of reproducing those actions toward our children. Our external actions are dictated by our internal imagination. Children who make inner vows will likely spend years imagining and replaying in their minds what their parents did to them. One way to change this is to change what we see in our imagination—as Jacob did when he changed what his flock saw.

The generations that followed Jacob's original sheep were also affected. If we are not looking toward our heavenly Father, we will reproduce what our fathers and mothers have shown us. If we change what we see or imagine, we can change how we parent our children. When that happens, our children will have many more positive and godly things passed down to them. They will not have as many unhealthy cycles to break in their lives, because we will have already broken them.

BREAKING CYCLES

We have had too many generations repeat the negative things they received from their parents. In some cases, the cycles never get broken. Time and again, parents have told me that when they find themselves in certain stressful situations they feel as if their dad or mom comes flying out of them. Without intending to, they respond and sound as their parents responded and sounded. Not only have I helped many parents who are in this situation, but I have found myself in it as well. I remember sitting on the floor at my mom's house crying and asking her why I was repeating the things that I did not like about my dad. The weight of my behavior had become more than I could bear, and I felt powerless to change it. I was saved and born again, but it was as if I was not in control of my own life. It was like I could not live out fully what God had done in my life, and I could only repeat what my father had done.

Something similar happened to the city of Nazareth. Jesus had come home and was teaching in the synagogues in such a way that astonished the townspeople (see Matthew 13). They were caught off guard because they only knew Him as the carpenter's son. They could not figure out where He had gotten such wisdom and mighty works. The Bible says that, "they were offended at Him" (Matthew 13:57). But when Jesus addressed their words, He did not call it offense. He called it acting "without honor" (verse 57).

The story concludes with, "He did not do many mighty works there because of their unbelief" (verse 58). In a few short verses we see the results of offense, of acting without honor and of unbelief: the city was unable to access the anointing that the Father had put on Jesus' life because they were only pulling from their knowledge of His earthly family.

Years after asking my mom why I continued to repeat the unwanted behaviors of my dad, I learned the definition of the word *honor* and the impact that it has in the spiritual realm. Bill Johnson says that honor "celebrates people for who they are without stumbling over who they are not."[1] At some point

---

1. Eric Johnson and Bill Johnson, *Momentum: What God Starts, Never Ends* (Shippensburg: Destiny Image, 2011), Kindle edition, chapter 4.

in life, people do not live out fully what God has spoken about them. They sometimes fail to act in ways that line up with the truth of who they are. These failures then, are what we need to be careful not to stumble over. Dishonor, or stumbling over who they are not, is what we step into whenever we get tripped up over others' failures to act in line with their God-given identity. When we dishonor, we blind ourselves to who God made that person to be.

I realized that for my entire life I had only paid attention to the failures of my dad. I had never seen him the way God designed him, and because of that I had never celebrated who he was. I had spent my life stumbling over his failures. I was in prayer one day when, out of nowhere, God showed me how my dad used to fly across the country, get off the plane to meet me, and then get right back on the plane with me to go spend time at his house. My dad would travel any distance and use all his vacation time to be with me.

When I saw this, it was obvious that while he had failures, my dad was also showing me Father God's heart for me. In a moment, I switched from dishonor to honor. Before I knew it, I was no longer repeating the failures of my father.

DOWNLOADS AVAILABLE

In the spirit realm, honor and dishonor are similar to what a download button is on the internet. The buttons we click online provide us with whatever is connected to the button. Some buttons bring malware onto our computers, while others bring movies or books. Some buttons will even clean our computers from previous downloads that were dangerous.

When we dishonor or are offended by our parents—similarly to how the people of Nazareth felt about Jesus—we download whatever is ungodly in the family line. In the same way, when we step past what they have done and see them the way God made them, we begin to download from His family line. We click a different button. When we repeat a failure from a previous generation it is likely a sign to us that we are in dishonor.

Since we are talking about downloads, I believe that it is critical that we learn how we store information in our personal "hard drives." One of my favorite movies is the children's movie *Inside Out*. It takes place inside the headquarters, or mind, of twelve-year-old Riley. There is so much to learn from the movie, but one thing that stands out to me is how the writers depicted how we store information that comes to us. Inside of Riley's head are five emotions: joy, sadness, fear, anger and disgust. Each emotion has a corresponding color. Joy is yellow, sadness is blue, fear is purple, anger is red, and disgust is green.

Everything that happens in Riley's life elicits an emotion, and the memories that come into her head come in whichever color those emotions represent. Her first memory of her family, for example, brought joy, so when the memory came into her mind, it came in as a yellow sphere. Other interactions with her family brought anger, so those memories came to her mind in a red sphere. What the movie demonstrates really well is that all of the information that comes to us is contained inside of whatever emotional state we were in as we learned that information.

When we read a parenting book, we learn new information. Oftentimes we are excited to learn new skills, tools and approaches to parenting, so we take all we read into our minds. Therein lies the problem. We take in the information from the book while we are in the emotional state of joy, so all of the information we learn from the book comes contained in that joyful emotion. Not only that, we only have time typically to read parenting books when the kids are in bed or when we are on vacation. Because of that, the information that we take in is digested while we are in a peaceful emotional state.

The issue is that we do not need the information we learned when we are joyful and peaceful. We need it when we are angry or frustrated that the kids will not brush their teeth or get into bed. We need it when we should have left the house eight minutes ago and they still do not have their shoes on or have their lunches made. In other words, we need that information to be stored inside anger, disgust or frustration—but not joy.

This is why many parents wonder, when they are trying to get the kids out the door, why the only parenting tool that they remember is what they did the last two hundred times the situation happened. And these tools that are accessed easily are typically ones that their parents used with them. When they are back in a state of peace, they are shocked to realize that they remember the tools they learned in the book. These are the very tools that escaped their brain when they really needed them.

I am not saying we should get angry as we read a book in order to store the information inside the emotion of anger. I am saying we can use our imaginations to access that emotion and watch ourselves do the things we are learning so that when we really are angry, the information is available and not elusive.

SWAPPING MAGAZINES

Another way to say this is with the word *trigger*. I am sure that you know what triggers are, and you probably know which ones you have. A trigger is something that when it is touched causes a reaction. Let's take the bedtime example, as many parents are triggered during that time. We want our kids to brush their teeth, use the bathroom, grab a book and get into bed. In other words, we want our kids to listen to us and do what we say. Bedtime is not really the trigger, but it is often when the kids pull it. The trigger is actually disobedience or procrastination. When kids do not obey right away, they have touched the trigger, and something is going to come out of their parents.

One way to think about triggers involves guns. Whatever magazine we have inside us and whatever is loaded in that magazine will determine what comes out of us when our kids disobey. In case you are not familiar with gun lingo, the magazine is the plastic, rectangular-shaped container that holds the bullets and gets slid into the handle of the gun. It is also what loads the next bullet into the chamber when the previous bullet is fired.

Just because we load some new bullets into a magazine does not mean we have that magazine in our gun. That is the reason the new information we learn in parenting books often only comes to mind after the stressful moment has passed. We may have loaded the magazine with something new and set it on the counter, but the actual gun still has the previous magazine inside. When our kids pull one of our triggers, we cannot figure out why what was fired so many times before comes out of us when we know that we should have reacted differently. Putting new bullets into a magazine does not mean that we also put that magazine in our gun.

One of the best ways to do this is to realize that our emotions are the magazines and our new skills or tools are the bullets. I can learn all of the new tools in the world, but if I learn them when I am peaceful, they are not loaded into the anger magazine. When I feel angry because a child has touched my trigger, no new tools will come out. The good news is that once we understand this, we are then able to load those new tools into the emotional magazines we want them in.

REPLACING THE MAGAZINE

God sends Joshua to lead the Israelites into the Promised Land. This is the land that they could have taken many years earlier, but they had not yet. God told him:

> "Only be strong and very courageous, that you may observe to do according to all the law which Moses My servant commanded you; do not turn from it to the right hand or to the left,

that you may prosper wherever you go. This Book of the Law shall not depart from your mouth, but you shall meditate in it day and night, that you may observe to do according to all that is written in it. For then you will make your way prosperous, and then you will have good success."

Joshua 1:7–8

In order for Joshua to take the Promised Land, he had to be strong and courageous. And in order for him to be strong and courageous, he needed his mind and mouth to be filled with what God had spoken. He would be prosperous and have good success because of meditation. Meditation is thinking deeply and repetitively about a phrase, verse or story. Similar to how a cow chews her cud, bringing it up over and over to chew it some more, we bring godly words up over and over in our minds to "chew on them."

Meditation will also make us prosperous and successful as parents. In meditation, we can use quiet moments to imagine scenarios in which we know we get triggered. We can sit at the kitchen table peacefully with our coffee and imagine what the bedtime routine might be later that evening. In our minds, we can watch our children do what they have done many nights before: avoid brushing their teeth and then drag their feet as they prepare for bed. As we watch this, we can also begin to feel the frustration we have had during the previous nights. As we feel that frustration, we are pulling out the magazine that holds the emotion of frustration. This feeling is important, because we want to store our new tools inside that feeling. As we feel it, we can then picture ourselves choosing and responding with the new tool that we want to use.

Instead of getting upset and raising our voices at our children, we can imagine ourselves telling them calmly that they are welcome to take as much time as they want to get ready for bed. Yes, we just imagined ourselves telling them they are welcome to disobey and procrastinate, and yes, this encourages them to pull our trigger. It may sound ridiculous, but they are going to pull it whether we encourage it or not. We imagine ourselves being patient, delivering a consequence and allowing them to choose what they will do. We watch ourselves remain in control instead of allowing our children's behavior to determine our own.

During this time of meditation, we should ask the Holy Spirit to empower what we have just imagined, and then go about our day. Later that night our children will do again what they have done so many times before, but this time we can choose to respond differently. We now have a choice. And when we start to feel frustrated, the scenes we watched will become available to us.

There have been many times that I have visualized a particular scenario in the morning and then encountered that same scenario later in the day. When I began to feel upset, the scene that I saw in the morning popped up in my mind, and the Holy Spirit helped me to choose the reaction that I meditated on. Since I had already seen a new way of behaving, I do not have to settle for how I have reacted previously. I am no longer powerless to repeat any poor treatment of my children.

We must remember that the behavior of our children is not a sign that we are good parents—our behavior is. If we talk to God only about the challenges we are facing with our kids, we are focusing on the giants rather than the available fruit. If we are watching scenes that we do not want, we are like sheep who have no choice but to reproduce in our children what was given to us from our family, instead of reproducing what our Shepherd has shown us. No one else can do this for you. No one else can choose for you what you allow to pass through your imagination. It is a decision and a discipline that we all have to choose for ourselves.

PRAYER PROMPT

Ask Father God to transform your mind and break any unhealthy cycles you have received from your parents. Ask Him to help you imagine how He wants you to respond when you get triggered. Ask for wisdom on how to love well and stay in control of yourself. Take some time and watch yourself act out what He's shown you to do instead of what you have previously done. Feel the feelings involved as you do.

6

DO NOT (ALWAYS) TELL THE TRUTH

Jesus told us that in order to live in freedom, we need to know the truth (see John 8:32). This also means that if we believe lies, we will not live a life of freedom. In other words, the areas of our lives in which we are not walking in freedom reveal where we are believing lies. We also know that one of the devil's primary tools is lying, since he is "the father of lies" (John 8:44 ESV). These are truths that we teach children in church, but because parents are the first pastors, we should also implement these truths at home. When parents understand the fact that they are the first pastors, they are able to let the church function as a support system to what is already happening in their home.

QUESTION THE LIES

Declaring the truth over your family is so crucial. I love declarations, and I make them daily over my family; however, there are also times when declarations are not what is needed. One of those times can be when our children believe a lie. Oftentimes, when we realize our children may be struggling in this area, we come right out and start declaring the truth to them. This can be very helpful sometimes, but not at other times.

There are times when the best thing we can do is to question the lies coming at them instead of telling them what the truth is. It feels challenging again for me to put language to how we can recognize when to declare and when not to, but this is when discernment is needed. If I have come right out and told my kids the truth and they shut down to it, then I need to ask questions. If I ask questions and they seem confused, I likely need to remind them the truth of what God says about them.

I had a conversation with a mom in which she told me that every time her son came to her with a lie that he believed, she would declare the truth that God had shown her about him.

She said to me, "I know exactly who God says my son is and what God has put on his life. As soon as he says anything scary or a lie he is believing, I make declarations over him." When I asked her how he received the truth, she told me that he does not receive it at all. He does not even pay attention to her during these times. I told her she may want to stop declaring the truth over him. Instead, she should take what God has shown her about her son and declare it in prayer in her prayer closet.

I am proud of this mom, because not only did she change her approach with her son, she also started taking this approach with her teenage daughter. Her daughter had been struggling, and as a result she had shut her mom almost completely out of her life. The daughter went from avoiding her mom and pushing back on everything that she said to being wide open and wanting to talk. She not only began sharing with her mom her struggles, but she also began to invite her mom to have an influence on how she thinks.

We all have times where our children (or spouses) are struggling with the lies that come at them. Most of the time our go-to solution is to come right out and tell them the truth about the situation. If our child says, "Nobody likes me," we often respond immediately with, "That's not true!" We might even follow up with several reasons of how we know that people like them. We try to convince them that they are wrong about what they are feeling.

If you have ever used this strategy with your children, you should take a step back to analyze how well it is working. Did they agree with you when you told them the truth? Did they come out of their emotional frustration and back into joy? Did telling them the truth work? We must evaluate these questions honestly. Most parents I have spoken to about this tell me that they speak truth to their kids, but it does not seem to help. Their kids either stay stuck in their struggles or shut down.

We have to ask ourselves why we do this if it does not work. Oftentimes, we are doing so because we are afraid. We do not always realize it, but in the micro-seconds between our children exposing a struggle and our replying with the truth, some thoughts pass quickly through our hearts.

"What will happen if my child believes this? How do I get them out of this as soon as possible? Oh no you don't, devil!" Now, please hear me correctly—there are times when we need to tell our children the truth and break those lies off of them, and there are times where doing so could only make the situation worse. In those times when you are not sure what to do, I would begin by asking questions of your kids, and ask the Holy Spirit if this is the right direction to go.

Imagine that the lie is like a railroad spike. When your child comes to you and says, "Nobody likes me," they are holding the spike up right in front of their heart. They have taken hold of the lie, but it is not lodged fully in them yet. Now, picture yourself with a hammer called truth. We think we can use the hammer to pound that spike away from them, but if we are not careful, we may drive it into them. This can happen because when they open up to us and we respond intensely, they can go into self-protection mode. The lies always feel true to them. Even though we know that we are fighting for them, our kids might feel as if we are fighting against them.

Not only might we drive the lie in by speaking the truth to them, we may also teach them that in order to get out of their struggle they need us to do it for them. If we are not careful, we will teach them that we do not think they are capable of getting out of this type of thing on their own. It is important to remember that when one lie is coming at our kids, you can guarantee there are others close by. The enemy's lies work in packs (to the best of their ability, since the demonic really struggles with unity). Your kids may have said, "Nobody likes me," but if we pound that one in, other negative thoughts, which are like rust or germs on the spike, can now infect and fester in their lives as well.

When we say, "That's not true. Your best friend who came over yesterday likes you a lot," other thoughts are waiting. These thoughts could come in the form of "I need my mom to get me out of this" or "My dad doesn't listen to me when I tell him what's going on." Then other thoughts come. "Why doesn't anybody like me? What do I need to do to get people to like me?" All of these are designed to deteriorate their trust in us and in themselves. The satanic agenda is to drive the lies deeply into their spirits.

On a side note, notice how the enemy often lies to them. The lies come in the form of first-person thoughts. The enemy wants to send our children (and us) thoughts that appear as though they are their own. This way, they begin to think that they are their own worst enemy, and they begin to take on these lies as an identity.

QUESTION THE LIES

If the answer is that we should not always tell our children the truth, what can we do to help them? We should question the lies. This practice can help them begin to get out of "the feeling brain" and get back into "the thinking brain." It also empowers them to recognize lies and to stop believing them. As we ask them questions, we are building in them a new way of thinking. In the future when they hear lies, the questions that we ask them now will pop up in their heads without our having to be there.

When they take the spike and hold it up to their heart and tell you the lies that they are hearing, ask them questions that will cause them to think it through themselves. Here is how this could look:

Child: "Nobody likes me."

You: "Nobody?"

Child: "Yes, nobody!"

You: "Are you sure?"

Child: "Yes, I am sure. Nobody likes me. They all hate me!"

You: "Who hates you?"

Child: Tells you the name of a friend.

You: "What happened? Can you tell me?"

Child: "He would not let me play during recess."

You: "You really wanted to play, huh?"

Child: "Yes, and he never lets me. He hates me."

You: "It sounds like that hurt you pretty bad."

Child: "Yeah it did, really bad."

You: "Sounds like he is hurting if he is hurting you like that. Do you think maybe he was having a bad day?"

Child: "Kind of seems like he is always having a bad day, because he does this sort of thing all the time."

You: "I wonder if something hard is happening with him at home."

Child: "Maybe."

You: "Did you already ask Jesus what He says about this? I bet He can help."

Child: "I didn't ask yet."

You: "Do you want to? Or do you want to keep talking it over with me?"

When we follow a process such as this, we are inviting our children to question the lies that come at them, and we are modeling how they can go about this process even when we are not with them. We are also helping them realize that there might be other factors, such as the other child's home life, that could be causing the child to be mean. It may not be about your child at all.

Not only that, but we are also leading them to ask Jesus for His input in the situation. As this is happening, there is no hammer of truth trying to hit the lie, but rather a firm and loving hand taking hold of the lie and wiggling it loose. It is very difficult for a lie to lodge in your child's heart when he or she can see it for what it is and when he or she invites both you and Jesus to take hold of it together.

There have been times when I have been caught off guard by my child's statement and had no idea what questions to ask. In those circumstances, I repeat the child's statement in a questioning tone of voice. If they say, "Nobody likes me," you can reply with, "Nobody likes you?" I find that once I ask one or two questions by repeating what they have said, it gets easier for me to find more questions to ask.

I HAVE THOUGHT THAT, TOO

Another thing that has helped me in these kinds of conversations with my children is to let them know that I have been in similar situations. Something freeing happens inside our kids when they learn that we have been where they are and have come out of it. The enemy loves to use isolation to trap people in their struggles, so when our kids realize that we understand them and we really do know what they are going through, they stop feeling alone in their struggle.

I have all kinds of stories from when I was young that I have pulled out in times like these. I have told my children about when some people who I considered my good friends made fun of me for being the shortest kid in class. I have told them stories of when kids threw balls at me when I was not looking, and the balls hit me upside the head. When they are struggling and I tell them these types of stories, I am able to pull them out of any isolation they may have been heading toward. It connects me to their story and causes them to feel known. Not only that, it also allows me to tell them what went on in my mind after those situations. By sharing my stories with them, I am able to help them recognize the thoughts and lies that may have been running through their own minds.

This has been a very powerful tool to use with my older son. Oftentimes, when I have asked him directly how he feels about himself or his friendships, he does not know. It has been a challenge for him to put language to the feelings that are going on inside him. My stories have helped me ask him better questions, which in turn has helped him discover the thoughts he has had.

I have told him things like, "When that happened, I thought maybe they really did not want to be my friends anymore. Have you thought that, too?" Or I have said, "When they said those things to me, I thought that I probably should not try to be friends with people because I keep getting hurt. Have you had that kind of thought go through your mind, too?"

I learned this from working with groups of children in church. Whenever I would teach this type of lesson, I would share a lie that had come at me after a painful experience. I then would ask the kids to raise their hands if they had ever thought that as well. Over and over, kids who had no idea what lies were coming against them suddenly recognized them.

From there, I would ask the kids to say out loud any other thoughts they had encountered that could be lies. Usually one child would say a lie, and a bunch of the kids would again raise their hands showing they had struggled with the same lie. "The temptations in your life are no different from what others experience" (1 Corinthians 10:13 NLT). This means that the devil uses the same tricks on all of us. He tells us all of the same things and does not really have too many weapons in his arsenal. He does, however, want all of us, our children included, to think we are the only ones having these thoughts. The truth is that we never are the only ones.

LET'S FLUSH IT

One of my favorite next steps in this teaching is to get some toilet paper and have the kids write on it the lies they have heard. From there, we have them go straight to the "toilet." Since it is difficult to send 100-plus kids to the restroom, we made a giant cardboard toilet that could fit over a garbage can. This way, the kids have something tangible to which they could connect this teaching. We even wrote the word *truth* on the flushing handle so that they could easily see that God's truth is what removes the enemy's lies.

We have the kids throw their lies into the toilet and ask God for the truth. As soon as we hear what His truth is, we have the kids flush the lies. This exercise helps the kids see his lies for what they are, and it helps them associate destroying those lies with something fun. It is a beautiful (and gross) visual of how God enjoys removing lies from our lives.[1]

We are not always going to be there when our kids are struggling. If something happens in school, we want them to get to the place where they are able to sort it out before they come home. Kids see toilets and toilet paper every day of their lives, and because they can associate toilet paper with not believing lies, they could be in school using the restroom and be reminded instantly of how easy it is to get rid of lies and the feelings that they cause. They could have been experiencing a difficult day at school, but one quick restroom break could set them free and help them reconnect to the truth that God says about them.

DESTROYING ENEMIES

One of the reasons that we often move directly into telling our children the truth rather than asking questions or telling them stories from our lives is because we feel afraid. We get nervous about what could happen if our children continue to believe lies—and rightly so. This fear is a layer that sits on top of our desire to see our children believe the truth. But we want to operate from that desire rather than from the fear.

By not rushing to tell our children the truth, we give ourselves a moment to move beyond the fear of them believing the lies and into our desire for them to believe the truth. "And not in any way terrified by your adversaries, which is to them a proof of perdition, but to you of salvation, and that from God" (Philippians 1:28). This verse is not talking necessarily about our spiritual enemies, but because we do not wrestle

---

1. For more on this topic see my book *Revival Kids 2 Curriculum* (Seth Dahl, 2017).

against flesh and blood, and since there is always a spiritual component to any adversary, we can apply it this way. When we are not afraid of the lies that come at our children, we are making a very powerful statement to the initiator of those lies.

Romans 16:20 says a very similar thing another way: "And the God of peace will crush Satan under your feet shortly. The grace of our Lord Jesus Christ be with you. Amen." Every question you ask that comes from a place of peace sounds in the spirit realm like the footsteps of Jesus walking toward your child as He is looking for a snake that He can trample upon. In the movie *Jurassic Park*, there is a scene where water is rippling in a cup because a dinosaur is approaching. I think this is a good visual of the above example. Asking our children questions and refusing to let fear have any place in our hearts is one way that we make the wisdom of God known to the principalities and powers in heavenly places (see Ephesians 3:10).

BUT I HAVE PRAYED

As I told the mom that we spoke about at the beginning of the chapter who confronted directly the lies her son was believing, we should not always fight this battle in the presence of our children. Another way we make known the wisdom of God to principalities and powers is by taking the truth into our prayer closets. Not only do the principalities recognize that we are not afraid of their mind games, but they also realize that we know the truth.

I keep track of the Scriptures that God has given me for myself as well as for my wife and kids. Some of those verses and promises even predate our children. I have taken each verse and formed it into a declaration prayer that I pray nearly every day. I pray them in my own personal time with God and over my kids as they go to bed. This way, even though I may not be confronting directly the lies that they are wrestling with during the day, they still hear the truth of what God has said about them as they fall asleep.

In the book of Luke, Jesus tells Peter the devil's plan for him: "Simon, Simon! Indeed, Satan has asked for you, that he may sift you as wheat" (Luke 22:31). When I read that passage, I notice that God will reveal to us what the enemy is planning. The following verse says, "But I have prayed for you, that your faith should not fail; and when you have returned to Me, strengthen your brethren" (verse 32). When God shows us what the enemy is thinking and doing, He also shows us what Jesus has already prayed over us.

Picture Jesus telling Peter that the devil wants to sift him. Satan wants to attempt to overthrow Peter's faith by rummaging through his life and shaking out anything of substance. Sounds kind of intense to me. But as I look at Jesus, He continues nonchalantly with "but I have prayed for you." He knows His prayer is more powerful than the devil's plan. His seeming lack of concern imparts peace to Peter. He sees that if Jesus is confident in His prayer over his life, he can be, too. I cannot help but think that as soon as the rooster crowed, the phrase "but I have prayed" must have echoed throughout Peter's entire being.

God wants us to know His prayer over our children's lives. He wants to give us specific verses and revelations to declare about them, over them and to the spirit realm around them. God says, "Ask Me of things to come concerning My sons; and concerning the work of My hands, you command Me" (Isaiah 45:11). I know it sounds almost wrong to say, but I do believe that God is saying He wants us both to know His plans on behalf of our children and to command Him about it. This does not mean we get to tell God what He should do, but it does mean we get to tell God what He told us to tell Him. God can do whatever He wants and needs with no help from us, but He does prefer to work with us and the words that we speak (see Psalm 103:20; 149:5–9).

Jesus gives us another example about making declarations over our lives as He reads Scripture about Himself:

> "The Spirit of the LORD is upon Me, because He has anointed Me to preach the gospel to the poor; He has sent Me to heal the brokenhearted, to proclaim liberty to the captives and recovery of sight to the blind, to set at liberty those who are oppressed; to proclaim the acceptable year of the LORD."
>
> Luke 4:18–19

He knew what God had said about the purpose of His life from Scripture, and He set it as an example for us to follow. This passage shaped not only His own life and ministry but also the lives of the disciples that He led.

We all want to eat the fruit of life. The way we plant those trees is through the words that we speak. "The tongue has the power of life and death, and those who love it will eat its fruit" (Proverbs 18:21 NIV). In order for us to be able to build our families according to God's blueprint, we need to speak according to His Word and His promises over us. If you do not already have Scripture verses about your children, I encourage you to take some time and ask God for some. Maybe He will give you a Bible character whose calling is similar to your child's. If you have verses that have shaped your life, include those for your children so that the life-giving words your Father has passed to you will be passed on to them.

As you create these prayers, you can pray them over your children whenever you pray. Pray these prayers over them before bed, keeping in mind that you want to focus on what God is doing and saying and not on what you are fighting against or the things with which you are dealing currently. You want your kids to go to bed with their focus on God and not the enemy or anything bad he is up to.

God does not want us going to sleep with negative emotions. "'Be angry, and do not sin': do not let the sun go down on your wrath" (Ephesians 4:26). Praying your verses over your kids creates an environment where they can have dreams from God, and it prepares them to fall asleep meditating on His truth (see Psalm 63:6). Having their minds filled with truth makes it easier for them to recognize when lies try to come at them. Believing truth is of absolute importance if we want to raise kids who are led by the Spirit.

Following the leading of the Spirit results in a life of freedom, since "where the Spirit of the Lord is, there is freedom" (2 Corinthians 3:17 ESV). And the Holy Spirit's mission is to "guide you into all truth" (John 16:13). Every time we ask our kids a question to challenge the lies, and every time we have them ask the Lord for His truth, we are assisting them in rejecting the liar's attempts to lead them in another direction. We are then empowering them to be led by the Spirit of God.

Dealing with personal lies and attacks helps our children be led by the Spirit, it paves the way for them to have a real and thriving relationship with God living in freedom, and it empowers them to see God clearly. Ultimately, the enemy's goal is not only to corrupt what we think about ourselves or other people, but it is to change how we see God so that we distance ourselves from Him. His goal is to cause us to walk away instead of drawing closer to the only One who can help us.

The next section of this book transitions into some of the ways our children can work with God to minister to other people. Having the ability to recognize who is speaking to them is important for this next step. Knowing how to look past lies to see truth and getting God's view on things is beneficial not only for our kids but for the people around them.

PRAYER PROMPTS

Ask God to give you promises and verses from Scripture for your family. Maybe He will show you a Bible character whose calling is similar to your child's. If you have verses that have shaped your life, include those for your children so that the life-giving words your Father has given to you will be passed on to them. Start praying these prayers over your children whenever you pray.

PART 3

SPIRIT-FILLED CHILDREN

7

LEARNING GOD'S ALPHABET

Speaking what God has spoken helps us build homes that both feel and operate like heaven. The Holy Spirit hovers and waits for the Word of God to be spoken so that He can create it. As our children hear us pray God's Word over them, they are being positioned to hear His voice themselves. We are to steward their connection with God. From that connection, they become kids who work with the Holy Spirit to have an impact on the world around them.

Hearing God's voice is an essential element in our children's relationship with God, since we live by every word that proceeds from His mouth (see Matthew 4:4). We live by hearing His truth about us. We also give other people hope by speaking His truth to them. We want our children to know how to hear God in all situations—especially when lies are coming at them. And we want them to see and treat people the way that He does.

Everything we teach our children about hearing His voice is easily practiced as they learn to hear His voice on behalf of people. Every time I have taught kids how to listen for God's voice, we have first practiced receiving a word for others. I encourage them to ask God for a word that they think is going to be for another person, but then I ask them to speak that word over themselves. In this way, they learn to prophesy over themselves at the same time that they learn to prophesy over other people.

My childlike definition of prophecy is hearing God for other people and telling them what He says. Prophecy is essential for our children to be able to bring God's love and power effectively to their friends and to the people in their spheres of influence. Paul said, "Pursue love, and desire spiritual gifts, but especially that you may prophesy" (1 Corinthians 14:1). Prophecy empowers our children to communicate to others the love that they have pursued. As we teach our children *how* God speaks to them, it is important for us to teach them that love is the first reason *why* God speaks to them.[1]

The Bible tells us more reasons as well why He speaks to us. "He who prophesies speaks edification and exhortation and comfort to men [people]" (1 Corinthians 14:3). Since many adults struggle to define the words used in that passage, we can be sure that kids do not understand. Let's make them really simple. The word *edification* means "to build up," and *exhortation* means "to call near." While we are at it, another way to define the word *comfort* is "to cheer up."

We know that in order to learn a language properly, we must know the alphabet of that language. We can teach our children to use the acronym ABCD. The letters represent the words Always Build up, Cheer up, and Draw near. As our children learn this prophetic alphabet, they will also experience something incredible with God.

1. For more on this topic see my book *Revival Kids 1 Curriculum* (Seth Dahl, 2016).

A second acronym that is good to use to help our children remember this principle is EFGH. It stands for how they will Experience Friendship with God and Heaven; therefore, ABCDEFGH is the starting point of teaching our children to prophesy.

We should help them understand that when they are listening to God it is like they are panning for gold. In order to find the gold, they must be able to sift through some dirt.[2] This means that there will be times that our kids will hear, see or sense things that are scary or that do not build up or cheer up. Sometimes our enemy will try to distract our kids with negative messages.

My daughter came to me one afternoon and said that she had seen visions of her brother in the future. I was excited to hear what she had seen, but the look on her face was one of concern. She told me that she had seen him becoming a bad guy as he got older. I was not surprised, because the enemy loves to attempt to interrupt children (and adults) with his word when they begin listening and looking for God's voice.

I took her over to the iPad that she uses to play games and began asking her some questions. I asked if she had ever been right in the middle of a game when an ad popped up on the screen.

She responded quite frustrated, saying, "Those ads pop up all the time!" I then pointed out that these ads typically pop up when she has defeated one level of the game and is moving to the next level. I then asked if sometimes the ads were for games that she wants to click on and download onto her iPad.

She answered, "Yes. That is how I find new games to play."

I then asked, "Do ads pop up sometimes that are for games or apps you would never want to play?"

She said, "Yes."

2. For more on this topic see my books *Revival Kids Curriculum* (Seth Dahl, 2016) and *Revival Kids 2 Curriculum* (Seth Dahl, 2017).

I continued, "Do those unwanted ads feel like an interruption? Are you eager for them to get off your screen so that you can keep playing?"

She replied with an enthusiastic, "Yes!"

I then told her that this interruption is what was happening to her as she was practicing hearing God's voice. God wants to take her to a new level in her ability to hear His voice, but the devil wants to interrupt her to see if she will click on and download his plan. Just like she cannot wait for those ads to get off her screen, she should see those thoughts or visions of her brother (or anyone else) in the same way. There are times, however, when God is showing our children something about a person who is not safe and they need to avoid. This is discernment, and is not the same as getting a prophetic word about a person.

If we agree to pay attention to those interruptions, we are tapping on a game the enemy wants us to play. If we do, it is easy to play his game and forget the game we were playing originally.

I then asked if she remembered the time her brother tapped on an ad and it took sixty dollars from our account. She remembered. It had made an impression on us all because we realized how much one tap of the screen could cost us. I shared with her that this scenario is what happens when we agree with thoughts that do not build up, cheer up, or draw people near to God. It costs all of us (the Father included) more than we want to pay.

I finished by telling her that not everything she hears, sees or senses when she is listening to God will be His voice. That is why it is critical for her to know why God wants to talk to her about other people.

ASKING MORE QUESTIONS

What can we do when our kids see something scary or negative about a person they want to prophesy over? We can ask good questions. There have been many times that kids have come to me with a scenario like this. Every time, I direct them to ask God what He plans to do about it. I have told the following story to teach kids how to handle a prophetic word that seems negative.

In this example, a young boy is giving a prophetic word to a young girl, and he says that he sees dark clouds around her, complete with lightning and thunder. His impression is that she is in danger, and he shares that with her. The children's pastor reminds him that God talks to us to build us up, cheer us up and draw us near. The boy asks the Lord what He is going to do about the dark clouds. Immediately, he sees a wind come and push away the storm from around the girl.

The children's pastor tells the children that whenever this young girl feels scared or as if she cannot see, God will come and clear the way to protect her. The children were taught that we should press into God to find out what positive solution He has in prophetic words that may seem negative on the surface. If we do, we will find how He intends to build us up, cheer us up, and draw us near to Himself.

Another thing to keep in mind when we are teaching our children how to use the prophetic gift is how to avoid unhelpful questions. Sometimes, when kids ask God for a prophetic word on behalf of another person, parents will ask them, "What did God say?" If the child did not hear anything clearly, the question can make the child feel as if he or she cannot hear God's voice.

If children think that they did not hear anything from God, it is oftentimes because they are expecting God to speak out loud and in English. Instead of asking, "What did God say?" we want to ask something like, "What is the first thing that popped into your mind?" This way, even if He chose to speak to them another way, they can still answer your question with confidence.

HOW GOD TALKS

As our kids learn how to hear God's voice, they will realize He has been talking to them much more than they may have noticed previously. English, or whatever their first language is, is not God's only way of speaking to them. He has many ways in which He communicates. The more they learn how to recognize His voice the easier it becomes for them to tune into His heart, mind and plans for the people around them.

In the Bible, the most prevalent language God used to communicate with people was through visions and dreams. It is simple to explain visions to our children by telling them that they can expect to see pictures and videos in their mind. The place this happens, of course, is in their imagination.

Some people get a little nervous when we start talking with children about imagination. Most of the time this is because they do not want them to be deceived. But we must realize that if we live in fear of being deceived, we already are deceived. Fear is deception. Instead of living in fear of potential deception, which causes us to avoid the imagination altogether, we need to teach our children how to use it. Teaching them about using their imaginations is like teaching them about any screen we have in our homes.

Take the television, for example. Just because they can turn the channel to negative programs does not mean we should get rid of the television. It means we should teach them which channels are safe to watch and how to tune in to those exclusively. We do not get rid of the computer because they can type in any search term or web address. We teach them, instead, how to make good choices about which terms they can search and about which sites are safe for them to visit. The television and the computer are not evil, but if we choose to use them poorly, evil can come through them. If we want to raise kids who are led by the Spirit, we must help them set their imaginations on His channel.

Another concern that parents often have is that since children are incredible at using their imaginations, they could make something up and say it was God. While this is possible, I believe that some parents are too quick to dismiss the possibility that God would use the imagination of children to communicate with them. The imagination is not evil, and it does not belong to the devil. God created it and gave it to our children. It is His primary means of talking to them, both for themselves and for other people. Since children are good at using their imaginations, they can easily learn to recognize God speaking to them.

Anytime I get into a conversation about the imagination with someone who is hesitant, I ask a few questions. Why is pornography such a problem in the world today? Why are children being exposed to it younger and younger? Why is the devil working hard to corrupt the imaginations of our children? The devil is not waiting to put things up on the screen in their minds, so why would we even hesitate to teach our children that God will use their imaginations to speak to them?

GOD SPEAKS IN OUR HEARTS

We all know the heart is an important topic for believers, and Paul prays that the eyes of our heart would be enlightened (see Ephesians 1:18). The majority of English translations use the word *heart* in this verse, but other translations use the words *understanding, perception,* or *mind.* In Luke, this word is translated as the imaginations of our heart: "He has scattered the proud in the imagination of their hearts" (Luke 1:51). The word translated as *heart* is also translated as *imagination.*

It is important to realize that our hearts have eyes, which means that we can see with them. According to the possibilities of how the word *heart* can be translated, Paul's prayer can be read as, "eyes through which our hearts imagine." The verse above finishes with, "That you may know what is the hope of

His calling, what are the riches of the glory of His inheritance in the saints, and what is the exceeding greatness of His power toward us who believe" (Ephesians 1:18–19). This enlightening of our imagination is how we know the hope of His calling, the riches of His glorious inheritance (both in us and other people), His resurrection and His ascension power. In other words, without engaging our imagination with God, we may be powerless orphans (because an inheritance is only for children) who have no idea why we are here (our calling).

HOW MANY CHILDREN CAN PROPHESY?

I was walking and praying for the upcoming service one night when a friend introduced me to a parent who was visiting from another state. This parent wanted to ask a few questions about how we trained our children. Within a couple of minutes we got on the subject of prophecy.

"How many of the kids here can prophesy?" he asked me.

"All of them," I replied. He stopped walking and looked at me as if I had lost my mind. He then told me that they had one child in their church who could prophesy. As soon as he told me that, God showed me in my imagination what was going on. As he explained more, what God had shown me made perfect sense.

His church had one child who had been singled out as having a prophetic gift, and they were grooming him toward his call- ing. They would keep him in the adult services so that when the Spirit came on him, they could hand him the mic to have him share. He started with something like, "Thus saith the Lord" in a really loud voice. I kept listening, while also grieving a little inside, waiting for him to ask me the next question.

"How did you get so many kids to prophesy?"

I answered him with a Scripture passage. "For you can all prophesy one by one, that all may learn, and all may be en- couraged. And the spirits of the prophets are subject to the prophets" (1 Corinthians 14:31–32). I told him that we create opportunities for all of the children to practice hearing God by turning their spirits to the Holy Spirit inside of them. We do it both in small groups and from the stage. We celebrate when they try (not only when they succeed), and we adjust them if they need it. Overall, we make it a safe place for them to learn to hear God's voice.

"How do you teach them to hear Him?" he then asked.

"Games," I replied. The conversation went quiet after that, and again I could tell what was going on. This parent was very serious about the prophetic gift—as he should have been. Speaking to people on God's behalf is a serious thing; however, God is also very serious about joy. We adults are the ones who must change and become like little children. We often spend the majority of our time with kids trying to change them to become like adults.

By playing games, we kept the process of hearing God's voice enjoyable. When things are enjoyable for kids (and adults) it is easier for them to learn. If we are too serious about moving in the prophetic gift, we can create a need for our children to perform. We want to be careful not to put them in a place where prophecy does not feel fun or safe. That can happen if all eyes are on them expecting or pressuring them to have a word from God. If the process is fun, safe and happens in an environment where others are practicing hearing God's voice, kids will walk away feeling positive about the experience.

One way we did this was to play what I call show-and-tell with God in small groups of about ten kids. We asked God to show us a picture for someone in the group, and then the group would share and discuss what we saw. If we were doing this exercise with younger kids, we would have them ask God for a picture of a building (see Ephesians 2:22; 1 Peter 2:5). The building could be a skyscraper, a house, a shed, a shack, a warehouse, a treehouse, etc. Once the kids shared the type of building God had shown them, we asked them why He would show that type of building. We also asked what the kids thought of when they saw those types of buildings.

Let's take the treehouse as an example. A child might say they think of fun and adventure when they think of a treehouse. Another may say that as the tree holds the treehouse up in the air, God is holding them up. One might say it is easy to pick fruit when you are up in a treehouse. Another child might laugh and say that he can only think of the *Captain Underpants* movie since the boys in the movie had a treehouse. These types of comments are very important for kids who are learning to hear God's voice.

It is helpful to ask more questions to help the kids interpret why He is showing them that specific thing.

"What did the boys in *Captain Underpants* do when they were in the treehouse?" I might inquire.

"Draw comics," a child might answer.

"Get away from school and the principal," another might reply.

"Why did they want to get away from school and the principal?"

"Because he didn't like them and was controlling them," may be the answer.

After we clarified, we would help the kids put the word together and then present it to the child we were talking to God about.

"God is holding you up and making it easy for you to get the things/fruit He is growing in your life. He is also making sure that you are free to have adventures with Him. He is making you into a person who knows how to go to Him when things are scary or when you feel controlled. He also says that, like the boys drawing comics in the treehouse, you are very creative."

This is a quick example of how a simple picture can evolve into a strong word for children. We have had many profound words come from the mind and heart of God through the mouths of children, all from the simple and sometimes silly pictures they have seen.

What the parent above wanted to do was something different from the process we were talking about. He wanted to train a young boy to line up with his definition of a prophet. In our church, we were teaching our children to practice the gift of prophecy. Even if a child is called to be a prophet from his mother's womb, our method of preparing them should always be kept age appropriate. Four-year-old children do not need the pressure of being a prophet to the nations. They need to kick a soccer ball and play outside, while learning how and why God talks in a fun and safe way.

Mary knew a lot about who her son, Jesus, was going to be. The angel Gabriel had told her (see Luke 1:26–38). To confirm that word, when Jesus was born, shepherds found Him and told His parents what another angel had told them (see Luke 2:8–19). What did Mary do? She kept all of those things and pondered them in her heart (see Luke 2:51).

Many parents do not have this much clarity from God about their children. If they did, though, they would probably do everything they could to make it come to pass. Mary did not try to force the words about her son into being. Sometimes, instead of putting pressure on our kids, all we need to do is treasure and ponder God's words in our own hearts.

PRAYER PROMPTS

Get together with your whole family and ask God to speak to you for each other. If something negative comes up, remind them that God talks to us to build us up, cheer us up and draw us near. Then have them ask the Lord what He is doing about any negative word that was spoken. If they need help, you can use the building example from above. Some other questions you can use to help are, "If they were a garden tool/musical instrument/ superhero, which one would they be?"

8

CHILDREN WHO SEE

I cannot begin to count the number of times I have been asked about what to do when children see spiritual things. "My child sees things at night" is a very common comment I get from parents. Most of the time the questions come from parents whose children are seeing creatures in their rooms, under their beds or outside their windows. Most parents start this conversation because they want to know what to do. As important as learning what to do is, we also need to learn what not to do.

WHAT NOT TO DO

One parent I talked to contacted me about her son. He had been seeing things at night for quite some time, but recently he had seen large wings covering the window in his room. It was clear from the conversation that she was not just concerned—she was scared. I asked her to give me any more details she could about her son's experience. She had asked him about the wings and what they looked like (asking kids for more details is always a good thing to do). He had said that they were white wings, and as long as they covered the windows, the black birds could not get into his room. The more she explained to me the details of what he had seen, the more fear she expressed.

For me, however, the more she talked the more excited I became.

"This is awesome," I said, catching her off guard. She was not sure why this was awesome until I redirected her focus to the facts. "Could the black birds get in?" I asked.

"No," she replied. "The angels wouldn't let them."

"So, your son has large angels protecting him while he sleeps so that demons cannot get in?" As she realized what I had described, her fear left.

Neither she nor her son had given their attention to God's protection, because they had been focusing on the enemy's attempts to get in. Even though the "black birds" could not get in, fear had. And this fear was the reason the enemy's attempts had not failed.

As soon as this mom became aware of what God was doing, her attention was refocused, and she was no longer afraid. She was able to see that her son's ability to see this was a beautiful and powerful gift from God. As long as fear was involved, the gift felt more like a curse. It prevented the child and his mother from sleeping, it altered their prayer lives and it required outside counsel. Focusing on the enemy for even one second caused far too much change in the atmosphere of their home. It was not the boy's ability to see that caused the struggle, but rather, it was how they were interpreting what he was seeing.

When our children see things that are scary or demonic, we must keep in mind that the enemy's first goal is to make us afraid. Why? Because fear is agreement with the enemy and is permission for the demonic to continue visiting. Once fear enters our hearts, we have opened a door for the enemy's second goal to be fulfilled: control. The real problem in the situation was not that her son was seeing scary, demonic black birds, it was that both of them were in fear. Fear about seeing demons is a much bigger problem than the demons children see.

KEEP THE DOOR SHUT

Fear is like an open door in the spirit world through which the demonic can enter. If we do not fear, their access is stopped. We must keep in mind, however, that the devil does not care about what is legal or illegal in the spirit realm. He is a liar and a thief, which means he deals predominantly in illegal behaviors. Even if the door of fear is not open, it does not mean demons will not show up. They will attempt to come in order to see if they can get us to open the door.

Imagine that your child calls you to his or her room in the middle of the night and tells you there are three weird creatures near the wall. This does not mean you should assume automatically that you or your child have the door of fear open. It could mean the enemy has shown up to try to get you to open the door. Too often, parents become afraid that they have an open door, and the fear that accompanies that belief ends up opening it.

If you know your door is shut, you can imagine that the demons are outside the door (even if they are in your child's room) pounding on it, yelling at you and trying to scare your family. If you refuse to open the door, they may still attempt to come back. If they do, as long as you do not succumb to fear they will eventually leave you alone.

WE WANT OUR KIDS TO SEE

Giving in to fear is the first thing to avoid. The second thing we do not want to do is to act as if the spiritual battle is not happening. Too many parents tell their kids that what they are seeing is not real or that it is just their imagination. There are, of course, times when kids make things up, but we need to approach each situation as if that is not happening. When we discount what our children experience, they begin to discount their own ability to trust themselves and what they are seeing. Simply because we do not see it does not mean what they are seeing is not real. It only means we do not see it.

Usually, our inability to see the spirit realm as adults is because we have focused more on the natural realm. We have grown up and become mostly logical. While we may have shut down our own ability to see, this does not mean that our children should. In fact, it is critical that they do not. If we dismiss the "monsters" they are seeing under their beds or in their closets and they end up shutting down their ability to see, it does not mean those monsters go away. It means simply that they are not able to see them. If they do not see them, it is much easier for the demons to influence them.

I spoke to a mom and dad whose son was having some pretty intense behavior challenges both at home and at school. We talked through how some of it could be testosterone, and we left it at that. The next time we spoke, however, they had news for me.

One evening the boy had gone into the bathroom to get ready for bed. His mom came in to check on him and found him crying right inside the door. As she comforted him and asked what was going on, he explained that he could see two demons. They were whispering about him because they knew he could see them. He told her that he realized these demons were the ones who had been causing him to behave badly, and he declared that he no longer wanted to listen to them.

The boy's behavior began to change immediately. His behavior at home transformed, and he began to do much better than he had been doing at school. While his behavior at school did not return completely to normal, his parents continued to help him remember the revelation he had received. We all need to be reminded of things God has shown us.

Before this event, his parents and I had focused on how to navigate the typical challenges of rearing a young boy before we considered the spiritual dynamics that could be taking place. When parents come to me for help, I look first at the natural circumstances. I believe that too many parents think their child has a demon before they have ruled out any natural influences. The last thing we want is for our children to think they have a demon influencing them if they do not. I have seen too many people think a demon was involved in bad behavior when it was a gluten allergy or something similar. When natural things have been ruled out, it is important to dive into the supernatural to see if there are unseen elements affecting the situation.

Imagine if this boy had been told that the things he was seeing were not real, and as a result he had turned off his ability to see. He never would have known what had been causing his poor behavior. Without that knowledge, his behavior would have been more difficult to change. Because the boy could see the spiritual forces at work and his parents believed him, they saw immediate change.

The opposite is true as well. If a child turns off his or her ability to see, his or her behavior can take a turn for the worse. Rather than turning off the ability to see glimpses of the spiritual world, we want to help our children develop this gift.

AGAIN WITH THE QUESTIONS

Being able to ask the right questions provides a major key for breakthrough. Not only do questions foster a good relationship with kids, but they teach them to think through, work on and sort out their own challenges. In other words, asking questions empowers them. Sometimes we do not realize that we disempower our children when we tell them what is going on instead of asking them about what they think.

In the same way, when we provide questions for our kids to ask Jesus, we foster their relationship with Him. If we do all the asking/praying instead of allowing them to, we can hinder their relationship with Him. I have found that when a child understands what they are encountering when they see scary things, they often do not see them anymore. They are able to take authority in the spiritual world.

SEEING IS A GIFT THAT NEEDS TO BE DEVELOPED

There are times, however, you and your child may face a persistent spiritual battle. Your daughter sees scary creatures, for example, and you come in and lead her in commanding them to leave in Jesus' name. They leave, allowing your daughter to fall back to sleep. The next night, however, they come back. Instead of getting worried or fearful, you should look at the situation as an opportunity for continuing education.

God does not want us to resort to formulas in times like this. It is too easy for us to believe that if we commanded a demonic presence to leave once and it left that we should take this action in every situation. Unfortunately, formulas like this violate the sense of seeing. Jesus did exclusively what He saw the Father doing (see John 5:19–20), and from what is written, He never did the same thing twice. If we do only what we did last time, we are no longer operating in seeing. We are operating in remembering (sometimes, however, God will remind us of something we did at a previous time to show us what to do in the current situation).

Every time the demonic shows up, our children have an opportunity to strengthen their relationship with Jesus. The more they go to Him to see what He is doing, the easier it becomes for them to go to Him on a regular basis. This process deepens their connection with Him. The more they do what they did last time, however, the less they go to Him. If they repeat what they have done previously, they can create formulas instead of relationship.

Teaching our kids what type of questions to ask will help them stay out of formulas and will encourage them to turn to Him. Let's imagine that last night your son saw scary creatures in his room. He commanded them to leave, and they did. Now they are back.

The first thing you could tell your son is that he should pick up his spiritual remote control and change the channel to God's. The process of refocusing children's attention to God is a foundational step. Sometimes it is good to have a tangible remote control for kids to push a button on, because it can help them connect better physically to what they are doing spiritually.

Then you should guide your son to ask such questions as:

Where is Jesus in the room?

What is He wearing?

Does He have anything such as weapons in His hands?

Does He have anything with Him?

Why does He have that with Him?

What is He doing with it?

The conversation may go something like the following:

Child: He is over by my door wearing armor and holding a sword. He does not have anything else with Him, but He is handing me the sword. As soon as I took it, the demons ran away because they did not want to get cut.

Mom: Ask Jesus what you should do with the sword now.

Child: He told me to keep it under my bed so that I always have it.

The next night it may be different.

Child: He is over in that corner wearing a hard hat. He has no weapon, but He does have a steamroller. He is getting in it and asking me to climb onto His lap to drive it over the demons.

Mom: Do it!

Child: Ha! Flat as a pancake!

Another night it could change again.

Child: He is right here next to me, and He is wearing shorts and a t-shirt and is holding a tennis racket. He told me, "Watch this!" and now He is running over and hitting the demons out into the darkness!

Mom: Sounds fun! They are gone?

Child: Yep! Way gone!

The important part of this exercise is that your children look to Jesus for the answers each time. This process strengthens their relationship with Him and reinforces in their minds that, instead of repeating what worked last time, they should keep going to Him for His guidance and intervention.

In the first account, the child was in a battle and Jesus gave him what he needed to fight. He showed the child how afraid the demons were of him. In the second scenario, the child got to work together with Jesus to flatten the demons. This scenario has less of a sense of seriousness and more a sense of fun. The steamroller is something used to construct roads, so it also has the sense that He wants to build something inside of the child. In the last scenario, Jesus did it for the child, showing him that this is a game He enjoys. The child got to see the true size of the demons (tennis balls) in comparison to Jesus.

These scenes are more fun and games and are not serious battles, but the results are the same: the demons are gone. There is not one right way for your children to have encounters with Jesus. The important lesson is that they learn to ask God why He is showing them who He is and what it could mean for them.

PRAYER PROMPTS

Ask the Lord if you have an open door anywhere in your life. If so, ask Him to close it, or ask Him what you need to do to close it. Ask Him what to do if something wants to open that door again. Write down what He tells you.

Ask Jesus what He wants you to do when your children come to you with something they have seen. Pay attention to how it might be different for each child. Take time to pray and imagine yourself responding the way Jesus wants you to.

9

EXERCISING OUR SENSES

We have been talking about the importance of seeing into the spiritual world and developing that ability in our children. They do not have to wait to develop these gifts. They can learn now.

> For though by this time you ought to be teachers, you need someone to teach you again the first principles of the oracles of God; and you have come to need milk and not solid food. For everyone who partakes only of milk is unskilled in the word of righteousness, for he is a babe. But solid food belongs to those who are of full age, that is, those who by reason of use have their senses exercised to discern both good and evil.
>
> Hebrews 5:12–14

There are several messages in this short passage, but the main theme is spiritual maturity. The author wants us to move from only being able to drink milk to eating solid food. He also addresses the truth that just because someone has been a believer for many years does not mean they are mature. He shows us that this is the result of being "unskilled in the word of righteousness."

If we are not skilled in the word of righteousness, we will have no discernment. Without the revelation that Jesus made us His righteousness, we cannot discern which thoughts are ours, which ones are God's messages for us, which ones are something the enemy is sending, or which ones are something we are picking up from the surrounding atmosphere. It is too simple to believe that everything happening in our minds origi- nates with us. When we know we are righteous, however, we are more able to recognize from where each thought originates.

THE WORD OF RIGHTEOUSNESS

The word of righteousness is this: "God made him who had no sin to be sin for us, so that in him we might become the righteousness of God" (2 Corinthians 5:21 NIV). Christ became sin for us, and we become righteous when we believe. We do not have our own righteousness. We have His. We are as righ- teous as Jesus is. We have been given a new nature, which is His nature (see 2 Peter 1:4). What is natural for Him is now natural for us.

We are like caterpillars who have been turned into butterflies in the chrysalis of His grave (see Romans 6:1–11). Forgiving our sins is what Jesus did *for* us—His righteousness is what He did *to* us. If we are unskilled in the word of righteousness, we cannot discern between the sources of our thoughts. We will think every thought that comes into our mind originates with us. I will never forget the day that I heard Kris Vallotton, who is a senior leader at Bethel, say that a trick of the devil is to make you believe the thoughts he sends you are your own. That one statement changed everything for me. I realized then that the devil had sent me quite a few thoughts that I had al- ways believed were mine. If we do not know this, then we will assume that everything we see, everything we hear and every thought we think is automatically ours.

When we know that we are the righteousness of God in Christ Jesus and that we have God's nature, we are able to recognize thoughts that do not originate with us. A mark of maturity is being able to determine if we are listening to a thought that originated in our own minds, or if we are listening to a thought that originated from a source outside of ourselves. If our children have no discernment, they can assume that the bad thoughts that they hear are their own thoughts. Shame, for example, can come in and tell them that they are bad because they thought something bad. If our children do not understand that this thought has come from the enemy, they are left to assume that the shame must be accurate. This sort of thinking is not only immature, but it keeps our children from being able to recognize when a demon may be speaking to them.

This is why being able to see into the spirit realm is important. If our children have scary or wild thoughts but do not have the ability to see the demons in their room, they could believe that those thoughts are coming from their own minds. If they could see the demon sitting next to them, however, they would be able to understand that those thoughts are being sent by the demon.

Keep in mind that not every negative thought our children have comes from a demon, and not every child deals with demonic visits. If your children are not dealing with crazy thoughts or drastic changes in behavior, then you do not want to encourage them to look for spirits behind every corner.

EXERCISE IS PROFITABLE

From the Hebrews passage referenced above, we see how the author not only focuses on seeing, but he also tells us that we should be aware of our other senses. According to the passage, we exercise our senses "by reason of use." The word *use* in this verse carries with it the sense of creating habits by practice. The word *exercise* is translated from the Greek word *gymnazō* that inspires our word *gymnasium*.

By developing a spiritual habit through practice, we grow in our ability to discern which thoughts are ours and which thoughts are not. The way to develop a habit is to do something over and over, and every time our children turn to Jesus to ask Him questions, they are developing the habit of turning to Him to get His guidance. We want our children to learn this with their sense of sight as well as with their other senses. If children feel a certain way, they could be sensing something from outside of themselves. If they have evil thoughts, they could be hearing something from outside of themselves. It is also possible that they could be smelling or tasting something in the spirit. This is not as common, but it is possible.

As we want our kids moving and exercising their bodies, they should also be exercising their spiritual sensitivity. "For bodily exercise profits a little, but godliness is profitable for all things, having promise of the life that now is and of that which is to come" (1 Timothy 4:8).

Think about what happens to children who spend the first few years of their lives running around barefoot, climbing trees and moving their bodies, but who spend more and more of their adult lives sitting at desks hunched over computers. Many adults are diseased and atrophied simply because they have been sitting for the last thirty-plus years.

This is what can happen spiritually if our children do not continue to exercise and develop their spiritual discernment. Eventually, they become the grown-ups to whom Jesus says, "You must change and become like little children" (Matthew 18:3). If we do not help our children exercise their senses, we could be slowing down their maturity and contributing to their becoming dull of hearing (see Hebrews 5:11). The sharpness they once had becomes dull, and the sensitivity they once had becomes numb.

If we only use the Word of God to show our children the lives of Bible characters without teaching them how to apply biblical principles to their own lives, they will have a difficult time maturing in discernment. The passage above tells us that just because someone has walked with God for a long time does not mean that they are mature.

If we help develop our children's senses and strengthen their God-given abilities, they could surprise us and other leaders the same way Jesus surprised the leaders during His childhood. "After three days they found Him in the temple, sitting in the midst of the teachers, both listening to them and asking them questions. And all who heard Him were astonished at His understanding and answers" (Luke 2:46–47).

FEELING AND HEARING

I am convinced that children come into the world with all of their spiritual senses functioning. I love *The Incredibles* movies. I believe that Jack-Jack, the baby, is a prophetic picture of how gifted our children are even while we are unaware. While we may talk primarily about people being seers or feelers, which can be helpful in understanding the way we most often see discernment practiced, that is not the only way we can receive spiritual information.

Treating children as though they are only seers or feelers limits their ability to develop discernment. If we met someone who had their sense of seeing, but who was deaf, dumb and could not taste or smell, we would pray for a miracle, because humans function best when all five senses are functioning. Our spiritual senses work very similarly to our physical senses. We must be aware of this so that we work to develop equally each spiritual sense.

As I am writing this, I heard something really loud outside of our front door. It startled me, and I felt a little afraid. The process of hearing a noise caused me to feel a certain way, which caused me to engage my sense of sight in order to find out what was happening. When I looked out the window, I saw that a delivery man had dropped a fifty-pound box of dog food on the front porch. Once I saw what had caused the noise, I did not feel afraid anymore. If I had not had the use of all of my senses, including my sight, I would have felt afraid until I was able to go outside and feel around for what was there. If I only had the sense of hearing and could not feel, not only would I be afraid from the sound I heard, I would easily get confused, not being able to find out what actually made the sound.

Knowing that, it would be both unhealthy and limiting to think of ourselves or our children as only feelers or seers. Often, we have one sense that is more developed than the others. It is likely that we are more accustomed to using it even though our other senses are functional. If our children tend to experience their world by feeling what is going on, we can help them exercise their other senses by engaging with them when they feel something. If they feel scared but are not sure why, we can encourage them to look around and listen.

I do this often with our older son. When he tells me that he feels afraid to go to sleep but is not sure why, we ask the Holy Spirit questions and look around the room. We listen carefully. We recognize that the feeling he is having invites us to engage our other senses to figure out what is going on and what God is doing about it. As we agree with the Prince of Peace, we feel peace in the room, and my son is asleep almost as soon as I walk out of his room.

If our children tend to experience their world more often through sight, we can teach them that their other senses are extremely valuable. The devil sometimes masquerades as an angel of light (see 2 Corinthians 11:14), so it is not always trustworthy to rely on our spiritual sight alone. This obviously does not mean every being that comes into our children's room that is bright white is the devil. There are several times in the Bible where angels from God revealed themselves in a bright, white light. Plus, if the devil is masquerading as something, then there has to be a real version of whatever he is pretending to be. Remember, he also comes as a roaring lion (see 1 Peter 5:8), but we all know who the real Lion is (see Revelation 5:5).

While it does not mean every angel of light is the devil, it does mean he will try to trick them. Let's say your child sees a bright white being come into their room. Immediately, they think it is good because there is so much light. When they tune in to their other senses, however, they will be able to get a better read on who it is. If they feel fear or hear confusing sounds coming from around the being, it will help them be able to discern whether this being is good or evil.

In the same way, Jesus can come dressed as a homeless man. If our children attempt to use their discernment utilizing only one sense, they may be inaccurate. This cycle of error may stunt or disable our children's maturity.

From biblical narratives, we see that people's first reaction to an angelic visit was often to become afraid. Nearly every time an angel encountered humans, he told them not to fear. These beings showed up and immediately calmed the fears of the people who saw them. In contrast, the devil will usually stoke those fears.

To help our children learn how to engage more than one of their senses in their attempts at discernment, I recommend you ask clarifying questions of them. When they see something in the spiritual world, ask them what it is saying to them. Ask them what they felt when it came in. Does it bring peace or fear? Do they feel joy or stress? Helping them process their experiences will help them tap into their senses and give them confidence in their discernment ability.

TRAINED OR TORMENTED

It is possible that if we do not help our children develop their spiritual senses, they may view the gift of seeing the spiritual world as more of a curse. I have a friend, Jenna, who is one of the most spiritually sensitive people I have ever met. She can see demons and angels with her physical eyes. She will watch a demon crawl up on a person and be able to hear what it whispers in that person's ear. She can repeat immediately to the person the thoughts that the person just had. She will then explain that it was a demon telling lies and that the person needs to break partnership with it if he or she wants to get free and find the truth God wants to speak to him or her. She has had this level of sensitivity her entire life, but no one was around her who could disciple her in her gifting.

While growing up, she could sense the motives of people's hearts, even to the point of having pity on people who were abusive toward her. Since no one told her this sensitivity was a gift or how to develop it, she began to self-destruct. She was checked into psychiatric wards nineteen separate times, and she spent years on multiple psychiatric medications. Those medications could not keep the thoughts and voices quiet, however, so she became addicted to multiple other prescription drugs in an attempt to quiet them.

Eventually, she detoxed through a Christian program. At first, she thought her craziness was part of her withdrawal process. It took her a while to realize that what she saw and heard was part of her gift. She opened up to a man who was leading a Bible study in her psychiatric program, but neither he nor anyone else knew how to help her. After the drugs were out of her system, she began to realize that it was her undeveloped gift that had been tormenting her for her entire life.

Once a week, they allowed her to go off alone to seek answers with the Holy Spirit, who taught her everything she now knows.

Her deliverance ministry began shortly after she started to learn from the Holy Spirit. She could see clearly the demons who were messing with people, and over time she began to see angels as well. Once she could see both, her methods of bringing people deliverance shifted. She found that if she performed an action as simple as hugging someone, demons would leave that person. She realized that, "Those who are with us are more than those who are with them" (2 Kings 6:16 NIV).

For over 35 years she had been interacting with the spirit realm but was unable to discern any of it. She thought all of it was simply in her mind. She did not even know there were people who were called seers until years later. She now realizes that all of her medication and drug usage was her attempt to numb and avoid everything she had sensed her entire life.

If she had been trained by someone, she likely would not have spent years being tormented by a gift that she now uses to deliver people from their torment. It is a beautiful thing to see. Jenna had to wait until she was an adult, and a very broken one at that, before she figured out what had been happening all along. Fortunately, our children do not have to wait that long. They can learn right now. As we train our children to exercise their spiritual senses, we are preparing them to live lives of victory.

RISE OF THE GUARDIANS

When I spoke with Jenna asking what advice that she would give to parents who are trying to raise kids who have a strong ability to see and sense the spirit world, she said that parents need to pay attention to their children's dreams—especially if their children have nightmares. If we do not help them process this experience, they can begin to feel alone and may try to handle the stress that this causes by themselves.

She cautioned that we need to remain patient in the process of helping them. If they feel that we are impatient or disappointed, they may shut out our voice. If they shut us out, they can fall easily into hearing and believing the lie that they are alone. They may think falsely that no one believes or understands them, or they may think, "I'm unprotected, so I need to protect myself." As Jenna and I spoke about her experiences, it became obvious that nightmares are one of the primary ways that the enemy introduces fear into the lives of these gifted kids.

One of my favorite movies is called *Rise of the Guardians*. Many Christian parents dismissed it when it came out because it has Santa Claus, the Easter Bunny, the Tooth Fairy, Sandman, Jack Frost and the Boogie Man in it. I was reminded of this movie as I spoke to Jenna, because the plot of the movie touches on helping children who are trying to process their dreams. In the movie, the Boogie Man used nightmares to destroy dreams, remove hope, alter memories and eliminate wonder, all so that he could prevent a life of joy and belief in children. Santa and the Guardians were there to protect those things and to remove fear from children. *Rise of the Guardians* is potentially the most prophetic movie created in regard to helping us discover what we need to be aware of to protect our kids.[1]

The devil wants to attack our children in their dreams because of how important dreams are to believers. The reason Jesus made it past the age of two was because his earthly father, Joseph, had a series of dreams (see Matthew 1:20–21; 2:13; 2:19–20; 2:22). Daniel helped guide a nation by using his gift of dream interpretation (see Daniel 2). Dreams also helped Joseph give direction to the nation of Egypt, and at the same time, his interpretation of dreams positioned him to help lead that nation (see Genesis 41). His childhood dreams also sustained him through extremely difficult times in his teenage and young adult years.

1. For a free message on this movie, go to www.sethdahl.com/guarding -innocence.

As a young boy, Joseph began having his first dreams (see Genesis 37). His family had no idea what to do with them. His brothers were angry, and his father was confused. Because of their inability to understand or guide Joseph through what he was experiencing, they made his life very difficult. His family did not understand the dreams until many years later. What if we learned how to help our children with their dreams? What if we could steward them better than Joseph's family did?

Nearly every morning as my children wake up, I ask them about their dreams. I do this as soon as possible, because I know that it is easy to forget a dream within a couple of minutes of waking up. I want to give them the best chance of remembering them.

Our daughter had a dream one night that she was leaving fourth grade and saying good-bye to her classmates in the middle of the year. Soon after that dream, we decided that we would move our family to Texas. As we were deciding what would be the best timing for the move—whether to leave partway through the year at Christmas break or wait until summer so the kids could finish out their year—we remembered her dream.

We brought it up to the kids to talk it over. With their input and our confidence in her dream, we made the decision to move at Christmas. We knew God was leading us through her dream, and at the same time He was preparing her to leave her friends. We have moved a few times since we have had children, but this one was by far the easiest for all of us. Had we not heard her dream, we may have made a different decision, or it may have been a much more difficult decision to make. We look back on this time as a family and remember how God led us through her dream.

MAINTAINING OUR ATMOSPHERE

One of our main assignments on earth is to live in the atmosphere of heaven. This is how we are positioned to bring heaven to earth. We live in whatever atmosphere of which we are most aware. Every time we become aware of what the enemy is doing, we are to direct our attention to God and His Kingdom.

You have noticed most likely times when your family walked into a store and all was well. Within a couple of minutes, however, you felt stressed or overwhelmed, and your kids started disobeying or acting differently. You have probably also had times when your kids came home from school and all seemed fine until one of your children became over-the-top upset at a sibling and completely lost it on them. Often these abrupt changes are because of unseen, spiritual interactions.

We are always interacting with the spiritual world around us. Always. When we take our children into a busy store, people are not the only ones who surround us. When our kids come home from school, their backpacks are not always the only thing on their backs. We need to be aware of—and help our children be aware of—the spiritual realm.

ANGELS EVERYWHERE

It can be easy for people to get so focused on negative things that they start looking for the demonic everywhere. You may have known people who can find a demon under every bush. We do not want that for ourselves or for our kids. It is important to remember that only a third of the angels fell with Lucifer. When that happened God still had double the angels. Plus, while the devil could not create any more, God could. It is possible that God has replaced the fallen angels many times over.

Because many children are sensitive to the spirit realm, it is not difficult for them to cultivate a lifestyle of looking to see what God is up to. One morning in children's church I stood in the middle of a line of kids. I had my eyes closed and was singing along with the worship leader when I heard a thought:

Ask the little girl next to you if she can see the angels in the room. I did not hesitate for a second. Oftentimes if we hesitate, we can end up coming up with reasons why we should not do whatever it is we have been instructed. I leaned down and asked her if she could see the angels.

"Oh yes! There's a huge angel right over there," she said as she pointed to one of the corners in the room.

Immediately I asked, "Why is he here?" She shrugged her shoulders and told me she did not know.

I said quickly, "Go find out." She left my side, and I went back to worshiping. A minute or so later she tugged on my shirt and told me she knew why he was there.

"Why?" I asked.

"For healing," she replied.

As the word *healing* left her mouth, I felt it hit my chest. It was a spiritual force more than it was a word that she said. I handed her the microphone and told her to direct any sick children over to the area where the angel was standing. We would pray for them there.

When the kids got there, we touched each of their shoulders and simply said, "Be healed in Jesus' name." We had them test out their bodies to see how they felt, and we found that seventeen children who had arrived sick that morning were healed instantly. One of our team members told us later that she could not believe how easy it was. We saw miraculous healing that day because of the senses of seeing, hearing and feeling. We learned that it is easy to bring God's Kingdom into the earth if we are able to sense what He is up to.

HEAVEN AT HOME

If you read my first book, *Win-Win Parenting*, you might re-member how I taught my daughter how to maintain the atmo-sphere around her by explaining the thermostat to her. Just as we choose the temperature that we want in our home, we can also choose the spiritual temperature of our home. And as we set the thermostat to create the temperature that we desire, we can do things in our home that will activate the spiritual atmosphere that we want. If we choose the atmosphere of heaven, which is righteousness, peace and joy, as well as the fruit and power of the Spirit, our children will know what heaven feels like—or as close as we can get on earth. If they know what heaven feels like, it will be easier for them to recognize when something is not from God.

Because we have His divine nature, we are new creations (see 2 Peter 1:3–4; 2 Corinthians 5:17). "As He is, so are we in this world" (1 John 4:17). What is true about Jesus is also true about us. When we know and believe this, we can recognize more easily when something is not ours. It becomes easier not to partner with the spiritual world. This includes when we are in a busy store and things seem to be chaotic around us, or when our children are tempted to believe the lies that accompany painful experiences on the playground. If we are proactive in cultivating the Kingdom of God in our homes, we will be less and less affected by the kingdom of darkness.

In order to maintain an atmosphere that feels like heaven, we must know how to adjust our environment to cultivate a heavenly atmosphere. And we must use every means possible to do so. I love having worship music playing in the background while we are doing normal life. There are times when the presence of God comes through the speakers and fills our home, and one or more of my kids will go sit quietly on the floor and encounter God. This cultivates the awareness in our children that God can show up anytime, and it teaches them how to recognize it when He does.

I also love having planned times of worship. We take a bit of time and come together to receive His love and to aim our love back to Him. This teaches our kids to turn away intentionally from whatever is going on and turn toward God. We cultivate heaven at home by both set prayer times and spontaneous ones. This brings our children intentionally into an awareness of God where they learn what His presence feels like in order to know when they are sensing something other than Him.

While these things are of great importance, we must also realize that these are not the only ways we can steward heaven's atmosphere. We do not want our times of worship to be limited to the moments when music is playing in our homes. We want our cooking, cleaning, dishwashing, laundry and discipline of our children to be worship as well. We do not want our children to join us only during our prayer time, but we want them to see us praying without ceasing. There are far too many families where the parents speak in tongues all morning and then yell at their kids all evening. Too many times we have compartmentalized our relationships and encounters with God without realizing that everything in our lives is a potential encounter with Him. We need simply to be available.

Another way we cultivate and steward heaven's atmosphere is by reading the Bible. I wake up usually long before anyone else in our home to spend time with God and to read His Word. Many times, God will open a Scripture verse or a story to me. I am often overwhelmed by what He shows me, and I will talk with the kids about it when they wake up or when we are in the car on the way to school. I have found that when we are driving, our kids are more open to the things of God. They ask questions, we pray, and we deeply feel His presence. I point out how it feels when God's presence fills the car, or I might ask them what they are sensing. In this way they are not only sensing Him, but they are putting language to what they are experiencing. Each of these exercises helps them recognize when He is moving.

PRAYER PROMPTS

Ask God to speak to you in ways that you are not accustomed to. It may be pictures, movies, Bible characters, creation or dreams, or it may be through hearing, feeling or smelling, etc. When God speaks to you, write down what He says. You can pray with your children and have them practice in this same way.

Ask God to give you wisdom to ask your children really good questions about their dreams and the things they are sensing. Does your family need help remembering or interpreting the dreams that are from Him? Does your family need help processing what they have been picking up from the spirit realm at night? Talk to God about your family's dreams and welcome Him into that area of your family's life.

10

WORD BECOMING FLESH

A few chapters back, we spent time learning about how God often speaks to us through our imagination. Not only is the imagination one of the ways God speaks from our hearts into our minds, but it is also one way we get the information that is in our minds to enter our hearts. Having ministered to children for many years, I can tell you that at least ninety percent of all children's ministries build their programs around two verses: Proverbs 22:6 that says, "Train up a child in the way he should go, and when he is old he will not depart from it," and Psalm 119:11 that says, "Your word have I hidden in my heart, that I might not sin against you."

We want our children not to depart from God's ways, and we also want them to live righteous lives. Both of these verses contain relevant promises for our children. Unfortunately, the majority of ministries have interpreted Psalm 119:11 to mean something more like this: If children memorize God's Word in their minds, they will not sin against God.

When we interpret the verse in this way, there is no promise connected to it. We must keep in mind that the Pharisees had the entire Bible memorized. Did they sin against God? Yes. Too often we have focused children's ministry on memorization of the Bible, when this verse is encouraging us toward meditation.

When I think about the Pharisees having memorized thousands of Scripture passages from God's Word it is surprising to me that they could not recognize God's Word made flesh when He stood in front of them and spoke to them face-to-face. They were so blinded by what they knew of the Bible that they not only could not recognize Jesus, but they spent quite a bit of their time planning and attempting to kill Him.

Contrast this with the man described in the book of Mark. Jesus shows up on the coast and a man comes running to Him. The man falls down at Jesus' feet and worships Him, calling Him "Son of the Most High." This is unusual because at this point everyone is still trying to figure out who Jesus really is. Obviously, this man was one of the few at this point who truly recognized Jesus.

> And when He [Jesus] had come out of the boat, immediately there met Him out of the tombs a man with an unclean spirit, who had his dwelling among the tombs; and no one could bind him, not even with chains, because he had often been bound with shackles and chains. And the chains had been pulled apart by him, and the shackles broken in pieces; neither could anyone tame him. And always, night and day, he was in the mountains and in the tombs, crying out and cutting himself with stones. When he saw Jesus from afar, he ran and worshiped Him. And he cried out with a loud voice and said, "What have I to do with You, Jesus, Son of the Most High God? I implore You by God that You do not torment me." For He said to him, "Come out of the man, unclean spirit!" Then He asked him, "What is your name?" And he answered, saying, "My name is Legion; for we are many." Also he begged Him earnestly that He would not send them out of the country.
>
> Mark 5:2–10

A man possessed by thousands of demons recognized Jesus, but the men who possessed thousands of Scripture verses could not. This should shake us deeply as we think about hiding God's Word in our hearts. We need to teach something more to our children than merely remembering verses with their minds.

Using our imagination to immerse ourselves in the stories of the Bible is one way we begin to hide God's Word in our hearts. My children always love it when I tell them stories. They want to hear stories I make up as well as true stories. They love stories of their mom and me, stories of when I got in trouble, stories of when I got hurt, etc. They love stories right before bed.

Most of their lives, my children have also loved it when I have read the Bible to them. As I said a little earlier, they did go through a phase when they did not want me to read the Bible to them. During this phase of their lives, story time came in very handy. One night as my children lay in bed, I began to tell them a story that went something like this:

"You and your friends get into a boat so that you can get to the other side of a lake. All of you grab oars and begin to row. Everything is calm, the night is clear and there are tons of stars above. On top of that, the water gently hitting the side of the boat is relaxing after a long day. As you listen to the water and row with your oar, you notice that the wind is starting to pick up and the water is starting to get rough. It is not too big of a deal since you are about halfway across the lake already. You are not really worried about it. But as the wind keeps getting stronger, the calm water turns into waves.

"You are in a small boat, which is never good when there is a storm, and this storm seems like it is going to be bad. None of you were prepared for this, so now you and all your friends are nervous. You do what most people do when they are in a boat in a storm: you start rowing harder. You want to get across the rest of the lake as fast as you can, otherwise you may not get across at all. Everyone is so focused on rowing that at first no one notices there is a person walking on the water a little way away from your boat. Someone yells out, 'It is a ghost!' All of you turn to see who could be walking on the water. Fear grips you. As if the storm was not enough of a hard ending to a long day, now there is a ghost, and you have no idea what it wants.

"Then the ghost calls out to all of you: 'Be of good cheer! It is I. Do not be afraid.' *No way can that be Jesus*, you think, but as soon as you think it, you also think about testing Him to see if it is really Him. You shout out over the sound of the waves, 'If that is you, Lord, tell me to come to you on the water!'

"'Come,' is all you hear from Him. You set your oar down and stand up, grab onto the side of the boat and step over into the water. It holds you up. You cannot believe what is happening, but you pull your other leg around and stand up on the water. *This is Jesus*, you think, as you start walking toward Him. You take your first several steps before you realize what you are doing. You then take your eyes off of Jesus to start looking at the waves that are still crashing all around you. When you do, the water no longer holds you up, and you start to sink. You yell out as loud as you can, 'Lord, save me!' And as you finish saying those words, a hand grips your wrist and you are as steady on the water as if you were standing on solid ground."

As I was sharing this story, I could feel the presence of God in the room. My children were fully engaged in the story with their imaginations, standing on the water as they recognized how amazing Jesus is. I, also, was wrecked by what I saw in my imagination.

Earlier, I had seen a picture on the internet of this scene that was supposed to be from Peter's perspective. In the picture, Jesus is reaching down toward the water and Peter is looking up, fully submerged. The look on Jesus' face is as though He is waiting for Peter to reach up and take His hand so He can rescue him. According to the Bible, though, Jesus stretched out His hand and caught Peter's immediately.

As I saw this altered version of the story, I realized that I had harbored an unrecognized fear. I had always heard—and even said—statements like, "When you find yourself in a storm, don't take your eyes off Jesus." It was as if I was afraid people would sink if they took their eyes off of Him. In reality, even when Peter took his eyes off of Jesus, He was there reaching out to him. I realized I had been afraid that my children would take their eyes off of Jesus at some point in their lives and sink. As I told them this story and had this realization, that fear left me.

The statements "My ability to catch you is greater than your ability to sink" and "Just because people take their eyes off Me doesn't mean I take my eyes off them" rang loudly through my mind. I realized I had put more faith in making sure that our eyes were on Jesus than I did on Jesus Himself. After all, Peter's head was not even under water yet when Jesus pulled him up!

INTO HIS WORD

I have loved C. S. Lewis since I was a young child, and I had the great privilege of visiting his home, pub, university and church during a trip to England. I will never forget standing at the desk in the room upstairs where he wrote the Chronicles of Narnia, praying to see the Kingdom of God like he did. I left that room and went downstairs, looked in the kitchen, then made my way down the hall to another room.

I heard the Lord whisper to me, *You missed something back there.* I turned around to see a wardrobe that I had walked right past but had not noticed. The Lord then said, *Many people have wardrobes in their homes and have no idea they're there.* I knew He was talking about the Bible and how most people, myself included, have treated it like a book instead of a door.

Not too long after this, I visited Austria to speak at a conference. This was the same conference that I mentioned before, where it was not the usual kind of conference for me because I would be speaking to both children and parents. During one of the sessions, I taught the families that the Bible is a door. I explained that we want to read it with our hearts and not just with our minds. I had everyone close their eyes and I read to them Matthew 19:13–15.

> Then the little children were brought to Him that He might put His hands on them and pray but the disciples rebuked them. But Jesus said, "Let the little children come to Me, and do not forbid them; for such is the kingdom of heaven." And He laid His hands on them and departed from there.

I read this story slowly to allow them time to really watch and experience the verses. It took about ten minutes to go through the passage. When I asked them to open their eyes, several children were weeping. It was obvious something powerful had taken place.

One of the girls hugged me, thanking me over and over. She told me that until that day she had never heard Jesus' voice, seen Him or felt Him. She did not just imagine Him laying hands on her, but she saw Him pick her up, hold her in His arms and speak to her.

I realized in that moment that many disciples are still stopping little children from coming to Jesus. While this is changing little by little around the world, there are still many children's ministries that are babysitting or entertaining kids rather than helping them engage with God. While they are not stopping children from coming to Jesus directly, they are not bringing them to Him. Engaging children's hearts with the Word of God is one way we let them come to Him. When we take our children into His Word, He might take them into His world.

LET THE LITTLE CHILDREN COME

On another occasion, I led children to imagine parts of Colossians 1:27: "To them God willed to make known . . . Christ in you, the hope of glory." They imagined Jesus living inside them. Within a couple of minutes, the presence of God was very dense in the room and a young lady on the floor started weeping. I could not tell what was happening, so I knelt down beside her and asked if she was okay. All she said was, "He took me to Golgotha."

Later she told me that Jesus had walked up to her and told her that He needed her to see something. He took her back in time to watch Him get whipped and nailed to the cross. As she explained, she had seen it all from John's perspective. She found herself beside Jesus' mother, Mary, holding her as her son was killed. When it was all over and darkness had overwhelmed her, she found herself curled up and crying all alone. At that moment, a hand touched her shoulder. She looked up to see Jesus standing over her. He pointed toward the cross and said, "I didn't do that only to take away your sin. I did that because I love you." Needless to say, that young lady was never the same. She had been through a door that took her into God's world. As Lucy found Aslan, she had found Jesus.

For this young girl, the Scripture telling of Jesus' death was no longer simply words on a page. They were, instead, words that had become flesh. The Gospel is part of her now. The love of God is no longer a sermon she hears or a song she sings, it is who she is. She told me later that Easter has never been the same for her. Whenever her pastor reads about Good Friday, she gets overtaken by Jesus' love for her.

I know firsthand that this encounter with Jesus has kept her from sinning against God. It is difficult to live in sin when you truly know what your sin did to Him. It is even more difficult to sin against God when you know what He went through to show you how much He loves you.

PRAYER PROMPT

Take some time to read God's Word and imagine that you are there while the story is happening. Do not rush this process. Let His Word sink into your heart as you encounter Him through the Scriptures.

11

THEY HAVE BEEN WITH JESUS

When our children enter the Word of God, they are learning another way to spend time with Jesus. They can enter into the stories of the miraculous works of God throughout the Bible and, when they do, they can begin to step into their own stories of the miraculous. From these stories, they receive faith to pursue the types of miracles upon which they have meditated. As they begin to see those types of miracles happen through them, the temptation to treat the Bible like a dusty old book full of things God used to do with people loses its appeal.

No one can take those stories from them. I like to say that a child with an experience is never at the mercy of an adult with an argument. You cannot convince young people that God does not heal today if they have seen Him do it over and over. This is why developing their own history with God is important. It sustains them.

In the book of Acts, we see one such story. Peter and John go up to the temple at the hour of prayer and come across a man who was lame from birth. When he asks for money, Peter replies that he does not have silver and gold. He says, "But what I do have I give you: In the name of Jesus Christ of Nazareth, rise up and walk" (Acts 3:6). The man was healed immediately. In the commotion that followed, Peter and John were arrested and questioned. They explained that it was because of the name of Jesus that this man was healed.

The people questioning Peter and John saw from them the boldness to stand up for Jesus when it was not religiously correct to do so. "Now when they saw the boldness of Peter and John, and perceived that they were uneducated and untrained men, they marveled. And they realized that they had been with Jesus" (Acts 4:13). The crowd saw both the boldness to stand up to these people, as well as the boldness that prompted them to tell a lame man to walk. The people around them credited this boldness to the disciples having spent their time "being with Jesus."

Remember that creating the atmosphere of heaven in our homes is important, and that the power of the Spirit is one way to make sure we are doing that. Being with Jesus is an imperative step toward cultivating the atmosphere of heaven both in our homes and in the world around us.

LIKE A BOSS

Having the boldness to heal the sick is the result of being with Jesus. Peter and John were doing what Jesus taught them to do and what they had seen Jesus do time and time again. Jesus told a lame man to "rise, take up your bed and walk" (John 5:8).

When we pray for sick people to be healed, we often do something that Peter and John did not: pray. They did not pray for the lame man to be healed. They told him to get up and walk. They understood something from being with Jesus, and that was that they were the boss of sickness.

My daughter and I were ministering at a conference called Tribe in Southern California that was put on by Expression 58 church. We were going through several verses in the Bible when I asked the kids if they noticed anything similar between the verses.

> News about him spread as far as Syria, and people soon began bringing to him all who were sick. And whatever their sickness or disease, or if they were demon possessed or epileptic or paralyzed—he healed them all (Matthew 4:24 NLT).

> But when Jesus knew it, He withdrew from there. And great multitudes followed Him, and He healed them all (Matthew 12:15).

> And the whole multitude sought to touch Him, for power went out from Him and healed them all (Luke 6:19).

As we all read these verses aloud, my daughter grabbed the microphone from my hand and said, "I'm seeing that Jesus is healing all. Not some, not most, all people!" I had not even arrived at the verse that says, "Also a multitude gathered from the surrounding cities to Jerusalem, bringing sick people and those who were tormented by unclean spirits, and they were all healed" (Acts 5:16). This verse was not about Jesus healing all people, but Peter's shadow healing all people! All sick people being healed is the type of thing that can happen when our children have been with Jesus.

When my daughter gave me back the microphone, I finished my message, and we let the kids minister to those who were sick. Many people in the audience were healed that day. Through these verses the kids realized that if God would do it with Peter, and He is the same yesterday, today and forever, He could do it with them as well.

Notice also that Acts 4:13 says that people "marveled" because they "perceived that they [Peter and John] were uneducated and untrained men." Instead of emphasizing merely biblical education and training, maybe we should emphasize being with Jesus, as this is what is needed for a Spirit-led life.

LESSON PLANNING

We kept these principles in mind when we created lessons for our children's ministry. We did not want our lessons only to educate the children, but we wanted to craft lessons that would lead the children to be with Jesus. We wanted them to experience the Bible more than we wanted them to know the stories in it.

For several consecutive months we taught the children using the miracles of Jesus in the gospels. We also brought in stories from more recent revivalists, because we wanted the children to learn that people other than Jesus did miracles. We also included stories from the lives of our team members. The structure of the lessons during this season was as follows:

1) Miracle from Jesus.

2) Miracle from a past or present revivalist.

3) A personal miracle story from the lives of the teachers.

What we would do each week as a team was come together, go through our Bible lesson and then search online and in books to find a similar story from a revivalist. We looked at such revivalists as John G. Lake, Smith Wigglesworth or Kathryn Kuhlman. From there we would pray and ask God to lead us to people in the city who suffered with similar conditions as the ones we were studying.

We wanted the kids to know that the miracles they read about in the Bible have been facilitated by other people, and that they can also happen for us now. We also did not want to teach anything to them that we were not doing ourselves. I would tell our team that we were not going to practice what we preached, but rather we would preach what we practiced.

One week, for example, we were planning to teach about Jesus healing the man with the withered arm (see Matthew

12:9–13; Mark 3:1–6; Luke 6:6–11). We mobilized to go into the city, hoping to find someone with a wounded arm for whom we could pray. Before we left, we prayed for specific direction. One of our groups felt like the Lord showed them three things to look for that would guide them: balloons, a white shirt and a specific local restaurant.

They drove to the restaurant and standing outside was a man who was wearing a white shirt and holding balloons. As they approached him, they saw that he had only one arm. Talk about finding someone similar to what we were going to teach from the Bible! They got to minister to the man. Even though his arm did not grow back, we still told the story to the kids, because we wanted them to know that God is more interested in faith and obedience than in results. By telling them even these stories, we were giving them permission to go for it no matter what happened.

During every lesson that we taught, we would point out how Jesus worked the miracle. More importantly, we made sure they knew that He only did what He saw the Father doing and only said what He heard the Father saying. Each time He worked a miracle, He was focused on God.

SWALLOWING UP CANCER

My family and I were at the Tribe Kids conference the following year, and as I was about to go up and speak, I was told that a young boy who had been in the hospital with cancer was coming to the meeting. The doctors had found stage four cancer in his left distal femur and thought they would need to amputate his leg. Miraculously, they did not. Instead, doctors replaced part of his femur and knee with an endoprosthesis in the first surgery. He was still facing surgery to remove cancer that had been found in his lung. He was supposed to have been in the hospital several more days, but he had recovered so quickly from the effects of his latest round of chemotherapy that they had let him out in time to come to the conference.

He came to the meeting that night in a wheelchair, thankful and excited to be out of the hospital and with us. As I finished speaking, I asked God to show me what He was doing in this young man's life. I saw a vision of Moses parting the Red Sea and Israel walking through on dry ground. I kept watching as the Egyptians followed the Israelites into the sea and the water closed in on them destroying them all.

I asked all the children to come to the front. I told them that we were going to be like the Red Sea and that the young boy and his family were going to be like the Israelites walking through us. As the family pushed their son's wheelchair toward the sea of children, the kids parted and made room for them to pass through. As they passed through, I asked the children to close in around them. We declared that the cancer would be swallowed up by God like Egypt was swallowed up by water. It was such a powerful few minutes—some of the most powerful I had been part of. The kids were not letting this young man leave with any cancer in his body.

Previously, the doctors had shown the boy's parents two cancerous spots on scans of his lungs. The doctors had told the parents that they believed they would find even more when they went in surgically to remove them. Shortly before the scheduled surgery, another young boy in their church had a dream in which he watched Jesus open his friend's chest and wipe out "sand" from his lungs. Then Jesus stuffed in bread, wine and oil into his lungs and sewed him back up.

The day of the surgery, the doctors again showed his parents the scans and said they would go in with their hands, because this type of cancer feels like sand. The only way to know the cancer's location was to feel inside of his lungs with their hands. They opened him up and searched for many hours but could find nothing. The cancer was gone completely!

DO WHAT YOU SEE HIM DOING

The main goal we have when we teach children about being with Jesus is for them to know Him deeply. The fruit of that intimacy is that they begin to know what God is doing so that they can partner with Him. We want to help them develop their ability to see, hear and feel so that they can sleep peacefully without fear, they can navigate busy and crazy atmospheres, they can understand the Bible in a profound way and they can influence their environment so that it looks like the heaven with which they have been engaging.

As we teach and encourage our children to minister to the sick, we want them to know what authority they have. We want them to know that they get to boss sickness around and tell it what to do, but we also want to train them to keep their eyes on Jesus as they minister. The key to a life of miracles is not knowing a formula or a model, although these can help them remember important principles, but rather, the key is knowing Jesus. We want to foster the type of intimacy with God that reveals His nature through their lives.

PRAYER PROMPTS

Ask the Lord what He is doing in your life right now. Where is He going? What does He want to bring to the earth through you?

Take some time to interact with Jesus. Think about ways you can foster an intimacy with God that is more than a devotional time.

PART 4
CONCLUSION

12

STAYING HUNGRY

Within the first year that I attended the Bethel School of Supernatural Ministry in Redding, California, Bill Johnson got up and said something along the lines of, "Anyone can burn for a school year. Anyone can stay hungry while they are surrounded by other hungry people. I want you to come see me in twenty years and show me that you are still burning and still hungry."

There are several restaurants around the world that are my all-time favorite places to eat. I have had many people tell me that there are better restaurants that I should try or that the food is better in other places. But once I have tasted something special, I am only interested in going back to that same place. I cannot be enticed to desire anything else. Not only that, once a restaurant has captured that place in my life, I want to try everything else on its menu. Before I even try a new dish, I am confident that what I will receive is going to be one of my favorites because it came from one of my favorite places.

At the beginning of this book I wrote about how the word *train* is used in Proverbs 22:6. If you remember, it can be translated to mean "putting something in the mouth" or "to give to be tasted." We want to facilitate moments with God for our children where they can taste of His goodness and "feed on His faithfulness" (Psalm 37:3) so that they stay hungry for Him no matter what else is presented. We want to be able to look back in twenty years and realize that our kids tasted something of God at a young age that empowered them to turn everything else down. This is my prayer for this book and my challenge for you.

THE GRACE OF GOD

We alone do not have everything it takes to help our children taste the goodness of God in the way I mentioned above. We need to get our kids around other people who are walking in different graces so that their unique grace may be imparted to our children.

I have seen enough to know that my wife and I alone cannot lead our kids into everything God wants to give them, but we can bring them around other people who can. We do not want them only to love the restaurant, we also want to expose them to the entire menu. This does not just apply to the miraculous. If we know someone who has a level of intimacy with God in worship, we can invite them over and let them talk with our family about Jesus and worship. If we know someone who is strong in intercessory prayer, we can have them over to talk with our family about the things they have prayed and seen.

We can ask ourselves simple questions such as: In what areas would we like to grow? Who do we know who is already walking in that? How do we get around those people to let their grace and passion rub off on us? This is one way to help our children (and us) stay hungry for the things of God. This kind of intentional practice will develop our taste for the dishes that are on the menu.

A group of children's ministry leaders from another country flew to Bethel to visit us. They wanted to set up meetings with members of our team to ask us questions about ministry. Unfortunately, we were all out at a camp and did not have a phone signal. We did not see their emails until Saturday. Since they could not meet with our team members, they asked if they could sit in and observe one of our services. We wanted to help them, especially because they had flown across the planet to learn something from us, but I had to write and tell them our service on Sunday would not really be typical. After a long week of camp with several hundred children, we were going to have a Sunday service that was easy on all of us—every kids' church needs some services once in a while that are more relaxed, easy and fun.

These guys would not give up. Since they could neither meet with any of us nor be able to observe a typical service, they asked if we would pray for them before they flew out. That Sunday morning, they stopped by our team's room before they headed to the airport. We did not go into an office or have a special prayer time. We stood in the doorway and laid hands on them. It lasted maybe two minutes. To use the restaurant analogy, they could not eat a meal at our restaurant and did not get to look at the menu, but they stopped by long enough for us to give them the website where they could look up the recipes.

It did not take long before I started receiving emails about the changes that were happening in their church. They invited me to their country, and I was able to join them and impart more gifts to them. Paul shared, "For I long to see you, that I may impart to you some spiritual gift, so that you may be established" (Romans 1:11). What Paul is saying is that we can pass gifts that we have received to others by laying on our hands and praying for them. "I remind you to stir up the gift of God which is in you through the laying on of my hands" (2 Timothy 1:6).

What began for this church when we laid hands on them and prayed had been fanned into flames by their leadership. Now, every time I visit them, I see that they have matured more and more. I have traveled quite a lot, and some of those journeys are return trips to places in which I have ministered previously. It is not always the case that I will see growth in the people and churches with whom I minister. Sometimes I even feel as if I am starting over with them.

This church is different. Every time I visited, they were further and further along. They were seeing things with kids of which we had only dreamt. One of the things they did was take their kids into the community to minister to people and businesses. They asked God for prophetic words for business owners and employees and then went to those businesses to pray. They also developed a culture where the children were involved in other ministries within the church, such as the healing rooms. We brought children into the healing rooms at Bethel, but it was only after I had seen this church do it. What started with my team praying over them and imparting to them what God had given us turned into my asking them to pray over our church.

I told the children's pastor that God had put in her the same anointing that He had placed in me, and I believed that she was going to start traveling and teaching as I did. Since then, she has spoken to more people than I have. She has incredible influence in her area of the world, and I have received as much from her and her church as I have given to them. This church was not just hungry once—they kept eating and trying new things on the menu. They stayed hungry for God, and this hunger has taken their children's ministry to some beautiful places with Him.

This church desired something more with God, and they pursued it for their team, their congregation and their city. Their hunger prompted them to go wherever they needed to go to get to the people who were doing what they wanted to do to receive impartation of the gifts. They have learned, received and stewarded well what they were given. Because of this, their knowledge and anointing has increased. Now, others are coming to them to receive what they have walked in successfully.

HOW I GOT WHAT I HAVE

Toward the end of my first year at Bethel, Bill Johnson came to my classroom and taught us about impartation. After he taught, he walked around the room and laid hands on everyone. I wanted something dramatic to happen, and I was expecting to be touched powerfully by God. Instead, as Bill prayed briefly for me and moved on, I felt nothing. I chose to go lie down on the floor, and I told God that I would receive whatever Bill had released. I lay there probably for an hour while most of the other students left.

There was nothing dramatic and I felt nothing; however, when I left the building that day, something was different. I noticed that when I read my Bible, I had thoughts that sounded like Bill Johnson. If you have ever heard Bill speak, he can say one sentence that feels like a summary of an entire book of the Bible. He puts simple language to large passages that makes them easy for anyone to grasp. Those were the types of thoughts I started having. Bill's prayer over me was not long, but I received a spiritual gift. Years later, a church from the other side of the world received a spiritual gift from me. Needless to say, I am forever grateful for the power of impartation of gifts.

STIR UP WHAT YOU HAVE

While there are times a grace and gift need to be imparted to our children, there are also times when they do not need anything more. The church I wrote about above did not just receive spiritual gifts and start "cooking recipes," but they kept the gifts stirred up in their lives. When speaking to the Romans, Paul said he wanted to impart something that they did not yet have. To Timothy, however, he did not say that. He reminded Timothy of what he already had, which was the genuine faith that was in him. He encouraged Timothy to stir it up.

We once taught the children a lesson from this verse. We had a "chef" who had prepared a giant pot of soup. The chef told the kids it was an amazing soup that they were all going to love because it had many good ingredients in it. We had someone come up to the soup, look at it and act confused. This person explained to the kids that the soup looked as though it was simply a pot of colored water. There was a little bit of a pleasing aroma, but it appeared as though there was not anything inside. The person began to walk away.

The chef stopped him, however, and handed him a large spoon. He told him to stir the soup and see what was inside. The person stirred the soup, and all the ingredients that had settled to the bottom now swirled around the pot. The aroma filled the room, and the person who first appeared as if they were not interested suddenly wanted nothing but a bowl of that incredible soup.

In order to keep our children hungry for both intimacy with God and partnership with His power, we not only want to expose them to more of His "menu," but we also want to keep the godly things inside of them stirred up. Every time we worship together, minister to a sick person, give a prophetic word to a person or talk to someone about Jesus, we are stirring up the gifts of God in our lives. As we step out and do the things that God's grace gave us the ability to do, we stir up the gifts that are in us. We do not want those gifts to settle down and stagnate at the bottom of our hearts.

PRAYER PROMPTS

What impartation of gifts have you already received? Ask God about how you can stir these up in your life.

In what area would you like to grow? Who do you know who is already walking in that area? Ask the Lord to show you what He has for you in this season and with whom He wants to connect you.

13

FIGHTING AND BUILDING

As we build our homes with God, we need to remember that He is the architect and we are the contractors. We must understand, however, that we are not only building our own families with God, but we are rebuilding also what the family was designed to be.

Whenever I think of rebuilding, my mind goes immediately to the book of Nehemiah. Nehemiah heard of the destruction of Jerusalem, and he did something about it (see Nehemiah 2–3). He pulled the Israelites together to rebuild the wall. As you read through the story, you see that many people were rebuilding in front of their own houses. As they did their part to rebuild around their homes, they were also playing a bigger role in protecting the entire city. In order to make Israel the mighty nation that He intended it to be, God started a family. Before there were lines on a map, they were children. We are not only joining with God to build our own families, but we are also rebuilding God's original design.

Before Nehemiah got started, some people heard what he was planning to do. They were not too happy about it. In fact, "they were deeply disturbed that a man had come to seek the well-being of the children of Israel" (Nehemiah 2:10). As we embark on this rebuilding of family, we want to be aware that the enemy is not going to be pleased with this. He has spent quite a long time trying to destroy the family, and he will not like it when you start building your section. This same enemy attempted to divert the rebuilding effort through intimidation and lies, but his plan failed because Nehemiah knew his plan and put the right people in place to allow the building process to continue (see Nehemiah 4).

While it is necessary to be aware that the enemy will not be happy, it is more important that we stay aware of God's protection of us. The name *Nehemiah* in Hebrew means "Jehovah comforts," and he is a picture of our Comforter, the Holy Spirit. While the enemy may want to stop you from building your family, he is no match for the Holy Spirit. The Holy Spirit will put the right people and angels in place to protect your family. "Those who built on the wall, and those who carried burdens, loaded themselves so that with one hand they worked at construction, and with the other held a weapon. Every one of the builders had his sword girded at his side as he built" (Nehemiah 4:17–18). God gives you the ability to fight and build at the same time.

A TABLE IS PREPARED

I have received a lot of questions from parents over the years, but one that I hear time and again is about spiritual warfare. I want to show you a few verses that will help you fight and build at the same time. One that is foundational is, "You prepare a table before me in the presence of my enemies; You anoint my head with oil; My cup runs over" (Psalm 23:5). Whenever the enemy is present, God has a table prepared. Before we stand up and battle, He invites us to sit down and feast. We need not go looking for a weapon until after we have picked up our forks. After all, malnourished and dehydrated people do not fight well. As we rest and feast on God's faithfulness, He anoints our heads with oil. His anointing breaks yokes and takes away burdens (see Isaiah 10:27).

From a place of nourishment and rest, let's look next at the following passage: "Let them give glory to the LORD, and declare His praise in the coastlands. The LORD shall go forth like a mighty man; He shall stir up His zeal like a man of war. He shall cry out, yes, shout aloud; He shall prevail against His enemies" (Isaiah 42:12–13). The coastlands are the edge of our territory. They are where our borders are. In other words, praise activates the border patrol of heaven. The enemy has a hard time invading lands that have God, as a mighty man of war, defending them.

The way I picture this is that God has submarines under the surface of the ocean. He is waiting to fire torpedoes toward any enemy vessel that poses a threat. I know there were no submarines and torpedoes at the time this verse was written, but it is a great picture to help us understand the strength of God on our family's behalf. From this verse, we see how powerful it is to aim our attention and affection toward the Lord when the enemy is trying to get us to aim it toward him. When we refuse to give him the attention he is begging for and instead put it on the Lord, He turns His attention toward the enemy. The enemy wants our attention, not God's. He craves our attention at the same time that he fears the Lord's.

Psalm 149 is another passage of Scripture that reveals to us the power of praising God when we find ourselves in a fight.

Let the saints be joyful in glory; let them sing aloud on their beds. Let the high praises of God be in their mouth, and a two-edged sword in their hand, to execute vengeance on the nations, and punishments on the peoples; to bind their kings with chains, and their nobles with fetters of iron; to execute on them the written judgment—this honor have all His saints. Praise the LORD!

Psalm 149:5–9

Our praise executes judgment on our enemy. In other words, a home filled with praise is a home that does damage to our enemy. "Through the praise of children and infants you have established a stronghold against your enemies, to silence the foe and the avenger" (Psalm 8:2 NIV). Even if the enemy is yelling as loud as he can outside our stronghold, the sound of praise from our children drowns out his noise.

IT IS TIME!

I was really excited when the movie *Incredibles 2* finally hit theaters. It had been fourteen years since the first movie in the series had come out, and I could not wait for our family to go see the current installment. I was anticipating being moved by the second movie, because I had learned a great amount from the first one. From *The Incredibles*, the first movie, God had shown me that religiosity does not want us to live powerfully. It does not want us to live in our true identity. It wants us, instead, to settle for a mediocre life as if we were normal people (see 1 Corinthians 3:3).

By the end of the first movie, the enemy, Syndrome, was attempting to deceive the planet. He was trying to trick them into believing that he alone could save them with powers he did not have. His goal was to destroy and replace the true superheroes. His reason for doing so was because, as a child, he had been wounded by the very superhero he wanted to be like. Sounds a lot like our enemy.

In the movie, once the superheroes were told they were not allowed to use their powers or live in their true identities, the general public forgot about them. The supernatural families were the only ones who knew the truth and had the ability to stop Syndrome from taking over the world. After this first movie, a very long fourteen years passed.

During that time, I saw clearly that God works closely with those who write and create children's movies, even though most of them do not know it. It probably is not the writers' intentions, but God gently weaves His story and messages throughout these movies. I have had many believers who do not agree with me on this, thinking these movies are trying to ruin our children. To me, though, it makes perfect sense that God would use this medium for His message. There are millions of children who will never set foot inside a church, so He meets them in the theaters.

In movie after movie, the gospel is alluded to. It is easy to find themes of death and resurrection, the choice of love or fear and the supernatural power of God and identity of believers in children's movies. After leaving a theater after one such movie, I felt the Lord impress on my heart that He also influences the timing of when movies are in theaters. That way, He can communicate a specific message to children at a precise moment in time.

He said to me, *My Word is eternally relevant. Even on DVD or streaming, these movies will communicate a particular message to people. During the time movies are in the theater, however, the message they hold is fresh bread. Pay close attention to what I am saying to you through them at those times.*

This is the reason, I believe, for the fourteen-year gap between the first and second *Incredibles* movies. The world was not ready until then for the message contained in the sequel.

There are many strong messages in the *Incredibles 2* movie. Toward the beginning of the film, the family is eating dinner and discussing the fact that superheroes are still illegal. Dash, the middle child, announces loudly, "We want to fight bad guys! It defines who I am." This is the cry of every believer, especially our children.

Shortly after this scene, a series of events take place that reveal a plan to bring the superheroes back into the good graces of society. The plan would hopefully help society realize once and for all the good intentions that superhero families have and how people are better off when supernatural families live their true identities and protect them.

In this sequel, there is once again an enemy, named Screenslaver, who is a deceiver. This time, though, she uses hypnotic screens to make people her slaves. She spends the entire movie trying to set the superhero family up to do her bidding, to use their power to help her and forever ruin their reputations. Her weapons in this battle were her screens. If she could get the screens in front of their eyes, she could get them to do anything she wanted. If she could capture their attention, she could use their power for her evil purposes. Fortunately, the family broke free from the bondage of her screens and stopped her.

While there are many messages that could be pulled from the movie, an important point is that the world needs supernatural families raising Spirit-led children to rise up and stop the enemy. No one else can do it. The world needs you and your children. You are the greatest heroes the world will ever know (after Jesus, of course). The world needs you to rip off any distractions that have been keeping you bound and preventing you from operating in the power and identity God has given you.

God is setting all of us up to take our true place in society. He is teaching us to discover and steward the gifts He has given to our children. He is placing us in situations for which no one else has solutions. He is our ever-present help in time of need, so we build what He intended for our families and, in the process, redefine how a family can function. You are not only incredible, you are unstoppable. You are raising kids who will destroy the works of the enemy, which will make your home and the world look more like heaven.

PRAYER PROMPTS

Ask God for the "blueprints" for what you are building with your family. Dream with Him of what it looks like for you to step deeper into raising Spirit-led children.

Take some time to praise God even if it feels as though you are in a battle right now. Write down promises that you have received from Him and meditate on them.

Seth Dahl is a writer and worldwide speaker to both adults and children. He is known for his powerful wisdom that is communicated through a contagious joy and childlikeness. With over nineteen years of experience working with children and being a children's pastor, Seth has cultivated a passion to help parents create a thriving family culture at home. Seth loves to empower families to build a strong connection that fosters peace and creates loving, happy families. Seth, his wife, Lauren, and their three children homestead with a large garden and handful of animals on a small farm in Texas.